ICKWORTH

Suffolk

THE NATIONAL TRUST

Acknowledgements

This new guide has been written by Nino Strachey, formerly Assistant Historic Buildings Representative responsible for Ickworth. The picture entries are based on notes by Alastair Laing, Adviser on Pictures & Sculpture. The guide is heavily indebted to the writers of the previous editions, to the research and advice of Jeremy Musson, and to the following for their help: David Adshead, Saracha Brand, the Hon. David Erskine, Katie Hawks, Dr Marcus Lodwick, Dr John Maddison, Karen Murdoch, John Phibbs, Gwyn Thomas, Angus Wainwright. Chattels accepted in lieu of Inheritance Tax by HM Government and allocated to the National Trust.

Photographs: Kentwell Hall p. 49; National Trust pp. 6, 47, 50, 51, 54 (bottom); NT/Ed Collinson pp. 32, 34; National Trust Photographic Library p. 22; NTPL/ Andreas von Einsiedel pp. 7, 9, 10, 11, 12, 16, 18 (top), 20, 23, 24, 26, 28, 29, 52, 53, 54 (top), back cover; NTPL/John Hammond pp. 1, 3, 8, 13, 25, 31, 41, 43, 56; NTPL/Angelo Hornak pp. 4, 17, 18 (bottom), 21, 36, 39, 40, 42, 45; NTPL/Christopher Hurst pp. 27, 30, 37, 38, 44, 46, 48; NTPL/Ian Shaw pp. 5, 35; NTPL/Jeremy Whitaker p. 15; NTPL/Oliver Benn front cover.

(*Front cover*) The Rotunda

(*Title-page*) A late 18th-century Italian fan from Geraldine, Marchioness of Bristol's collection on display on the Museum Landing

(*Back cover*) Geraldine, Marchioness of Bristol's collection of silver fish in the Museum Room

(*Opposite*) Detail of the mural decoration in the Pompeian Room

CONTENTS

ICKWORTH

'*The House – The House – The House.*' So ended a letter written by Frederick, 4th Earl of Bristol and Bishop of Derry from his sick-bed in Naples in 1796. Although a thousand miles from Ickworth, the Earl-Bishop was obsessed by his new creation, which was inspired by the monuments of Rome. With its extraordinary central Rotunda and curving wings, the house perfectly expresses his eccentric personality. Katherine Wilmot called the Earl-Bishop 'one of the greatest curiosities alive', and his behaviour could be unpredictable. He once tipped a tureen of spaghetti over a procession of the Blessed Sacrament, because he had 'a particular aversion to the tinkling of bells'.

The Earl-Bishop with Mount Vesuvius in the distance; by Elisabeth Vigée-Lebrun, 1790 (Drawing Room)

Seen more often in Italy than in Derry or Suffolk, the Earl-Bishop used the income from his church estates to fund his passions for travel, for building, and for collecting works of art. Condemned by his wife as a 'stupendous monument of folly', Ickworth was intended to display treasures gathered during 30 years of continental travel rather than to be a comfortable home.

Designs prepared in Italy by Mario Asprucci the Younger were adapted for the English climate by Francis Sandys, a young architect who had worked for the Earl-Bishop in Ireland. Foundations for the new house were laid in 1795, and building work was progressing well, when, in 1798, Lord Bristol's magnificent collections were captured by invading Napoleonic troops in Rome. The Earl-Bishop spent the rest of his life abroad, campaigning fruitlessly for the return of his collection, and died in 1803 without ever seeing Ickworth completed.

Although the present house was not begun until 1795, the Hervey family (pronounced 'Harvey') had owned the estate since the middle of the 15th century. Early generations of Herveys lived in a Tudor manor house near Ickworth church, known as Ickworth Hall, which was demolished about 1702 by John, 1st Earl of Bristol.

Lord Bristol fully intended to build a new family seat on the site of the old hall, and obtained plans from two well-known architects, William Talman and Sir John Vanbrugh. Quite why neither of these schemes was ever achieved remains something of a mystery. Instead, the 1st Earl adapted a modest farmhouse on the estate, now known as Ickworth Lodge, which was to remain the family home until 1829.

The exterior of the Earl-Bishop's Rotunda was virtually finished when he died in 1803, but the interior was still an empty shell, and the curving corridors and wings only a few feet above ground.

The Rotunda from the Entrance Drive

It was left to the Earl-Bishop's son, the future 1st Marquess of Bristol, to make what use he could of his father's extraordinary plan. Having no need for massive galleries, in 1821 he instructed his architect, John Field, to redesign the East Wing as family living-quarters. Field fitted out the ground floor of the Rotunda as state rooms in an austere Regency style, with furnishings made almost exclusively by Banting, France & Co. The West Wing was added purely for symmetry and so was left empty. The Pompeian Room was decorated by J. D. Crace in 1879, and the last major alterations were made in 1909–11, when the 4th Marquess commissioned A. C. Blomfield to remodel the Entrance Hall and Staircase. The house, with much of its collections of family portraits, Huguenot silver, Regency furniture and china, and part of the ancient deer-park, passed to the National Trust in 1956.

As the family lived mostly in the East Wing, the rooms that visitors see in the Rotunda spent much of the year under dust sheets, coming into their own mainly for parties and other special occasions. But as a result, their superb furnishings and decoration have survived in excellent condition and little changed since the heyday of the house in the Edwardian era.

TOUR OF THE HOUSE

The Exterior

THE ENTRANCE FRONT

Over 180 metres long, the entrance front is dominated by the massive Rotunda, designed for the Earl-Bishop in 1794–5 by Mario Asprucci the Younger and Francis Sandys.

FRIEZES

The stucco panels within the portico were designed by the Earl-Bishop's granddaughter, Lady Caroline Wharncliffe, and depict scenes from the ancient Olympic Games. The remainder of the scheme was based on Flaxman's illustrations to Homer's *Iliad* and *Odyssey*, and was modelled in terracotta by the Carabelli brothers, Casimiro and Donato, who had previously worked on Milan Cathedral. The small section of the upper frieze left unfinished at the Earl-Bishop's death in 1803 was completed in Coade stone in the 1820s.

This section of the Rotunda frieze depicts the ancient Olympic Games

The Interior

THE ENTRANCE HALL

John Field's classical Entrance Hall, with its giant porphyry scagliola columns and black marble fireplace, was completed for the 1st Marquess in 1827. In the original design the staircase was screened from the hall by a thick dividing wall, against which stood Flaxman's huge marble group, *The Fury of Athamas*. When the staircase was remodelled for the 4th Marquess in 1909–11, the architect A. C. Blomfield chose to break down the wall, inserting a second pair of giant columns as supports, and moving *Athamas* to the rear of the newly visible Staircase Hall.

PICTURES

A handlist describing all the pictures is available separately.

FIREPLACE WALL:

61 ENGLISH SCHOOL, *c.*1805
Frederick, 4th Earl of Bristol and Bishop of Derry (1730–1803)
Traveller, builder and patron of the arts, the eccentric Earl-Bishop was the creator of the present Ickworth. Since the portrait is English and shows him in old age, when he was living abroad, it was probably painted posthumously.

WALL OPPOSITE FIREPLACE:

88 JEAN-BAPTISTE VAN LOO (1684–1745)
John, Lord Hervey (1696–1743), 1741
The second son of the 1st Earl. An intimate of Queen Caroline and a prominent Whig politician, famous for his scandalous memoirs of life at the court of George II, he is shown holding his purse of office as Lord Privy Seal, which hangs below, with that of his son, who held the same position under George III.

(Opposite page)   The Entrance Hall

SCULPTURE

FLANKING ENTRANCE DOOR:

A pair of giant busts of Hercules and the Roman Emperor Lucius Verus; copies after the Antique originals in Naples and the Borghese collection. On scagliola pedestals supplied by Banting, France & Co. in 1829.

ON MANTELPIECE:

HUBERT LE SUEUR (*c.*1580–*c.*1658)
A bronze equestrian statuette of Charles I; a reduction of the full-size bronze (now in Trafalgar Square).

ON TABLE OPPOSITE FIREPLACE:

EDMUND COTTERILL (1795–1858)
A bronze equestrian statuette of the Duke of Wellington (1769–1852).

BY DOOR TO EAST CORRIDOR:

A bust of John, Lord Hervey (1696–1743); copied from the original marble by Bouchardon, which is in a private collection.

BY DOOR TO WEST CORRIDOR:

MICHAEL WAGMÜLLER (1839–81), 1870
A bust of George Wythes (1811–83), the great Victorian public works contractor, whose granddaughter married the 4th Marquess and was largely responsible for the extensive alterations to the house in 1909–11.

FURNITURE

ROUND WALLS OF ROOM:

A set of hall-chairs, painted with the Bristol crest, supplied by Banting, France & Co. in 1829.

OPPOSITE FIREPLACE:

The massive oak table with white marble top was supplied by Banting, France & Co. in 1829.

TO REAR OF ROOM:

The pair of Venetian mirrors with pastoral figures engraved on glass is 18th-century.

CERAMICS

ON MANTELPIECE:

A pair of Chinese Dogs of Fo, 19th-century. Used to decorate the entrance steps of Buddhist temples.

John, Lord Hervey's purse of office as Lord Privy Seal

THE STAIRCASE HALL

The present Staircase Hall represents an intriguing combination of John Field's original design for the 1st Marquess and the alterations introduced by A.C.Blomfield for the 4th Marquess in 1909–11. Field chose to erect a simple stone staircase, with an elaborate cast-iron balustrade, rising around the four walls of the central space, and lit by a delicate glass skylight supported on marbled columns. Blomfield retained the skylight and part of the balustrading, but replaced the central stair by oak steps concealed within the staircase walls, linked by a single balcony. Blomfield also installed the decorative marble floor at the base of the stairs.

PICTURES

MAIN WALL ABOVE BALCONY:

JUAN ANTONIO RIBERA (1779–1860) after
DOMENICHINO (1581–1641)
The Last Communion of St Jerome, 1808
The original was looted from the Vatican by Napoleon and until 1815 remained in Paris, where

this full-size copy was painted for his brother, Joseph Bonaparte, when King of Spain (1808–13).

52 Attributed to ENOCH SEEMAN (1694/5–1744)
Elizabeth Felton, Countess of Bristol (1676–1741)
In 1696 she married the 1st Earl as his second wife, and had sixteen children by him.

84 Attributed to ENOCH SEEMAN (1694/5–1744)
John, 1st Earl of Bristol (1665–1751)
Founder of the family's 18th-century fortunes, he dramatically expanded the Hervey estates by marrying two heiresses: Isabella Carr and Elizabeth Felton. Having made his name at court as a Whig supporter of the Hanoverian succession, he retired to Ickworth after his elevation to the Earldom in 1714. Painted in 1738, but based on Kneller's likeness of him as a much younger man.

SCULPTURE

JOHN FLAXMAN (1755–1826)
The Fury of Athamas
Colossal marble group, commissioned by the Earl-Bishop in Rome in 1790 for £600. It represents the scene from Ovid's *Metamorphoses* when Athamas, driven mad by the gods, snatches his infant son Learchus from the arms of his mortal mother Ino, and dashes out his brains upon a rock, watched in terror by their other child, Melicertes. The sculpture was confiscated by the French in 1798, and

The Fury of Athamas; by John Flaxman (Staircase Hall)

bought back by the 1st Marquess in Paris in the early 1820s.

FURNITURE

IN ARCADES:

A pair of sedan chairs, early 18th-century. The chair on the left-hand side belonged to the 1st Earl's second wife, Elizabeth Felton, who is reported to have died in it while being carried through St James's Park in May 1741.

A porter's chair, 18th-century. From the Bristols' London house, 6 St James's Square.

THE DINING ROOM

The enormous height of this room, and the adjoining Library and Drawing Room, was dictated by the Earl-Bishop, who claimed that his 'lungs played more freely' and his 'spirits spontaneously rose much higher, in lofty rooms than in low ones, where the atmosphere is too much tainted with ... our own bodies'. The decoration and furnishing were carried out for the 1st Marquess in 1824–9; the Ionic cornice, derived from the Temple of Minerva at Athens, the simple door frames and solid mahogany doors and window surrounds were all designed by John Field.

CHIMNEYPIECE

The late 18th-century marble chimneypiece may be one of the few Italian acquisitions of the Earl-Bishop to reach Ickworth after his death. Like the more elaborate chimneypiece in the adjoining Library, it may have been amongst the 'certain chimney pieces marbles etc late belonging to the late Frederick, Earl of Bristol' stored in a London warehouse until 1812, when they were sent to Ickworth.

PICTURES

FIREPLACE WALL:

123 Sir THOMAS LAWRENCE, PRA (1769–1830) and Studio
Robert Banks Jenkinson, 2nd Earl of Liverpool (1770–1828)
Tory Prime Minister in 1812–27 and husband of the 1st Marquess's favourite sister, Louisa. Commissioned soon after his death by his brother-in-law, and inscribed in Latin: 'A happy simplicity which

The Dining Room

shuns the difficult journeys of speculation and follows the level and firm path of God's precepts.'

126 Sir FRANCIS GRANT, PRA (1803–78)
Lady Katherine Manners, Countess Jermyn (d.1848)
Married Frederick Hervey, Earl Jermyn in 1830, but died of smallpox eleven years before he succeeded as 2nd Marquess.

66 JOHN HOPPNER, RA (1758–1810)
Frederick William, 1st Marquess of Bristol
(1769–1859)
In character, the complete opposite of his eccentric father, the Earl-Bishop, whom he succeeded in 1803. He completed the unfinished interiors of the Rotunda in the 1820s, and built the East and West Wings with their long curving corridors. Ickworth appears in the distance.

70 Sir FRANCIS GRANT, PRA (1803–78)
Frederick William, 2nd Marquess of Bristol (1800–64)
The eldest son of the 1st Marquess, Frederick spent many years assisting his father with the endless building works at Ickworth, before succeeding to the estate in 1859.

65 Sir THOMAS LAWRENCE, PRA (1769–1830)
Frederick William, 1st Marquess of Bristol
(1769–1859)
Probably completed in 1827–8.

WALL LEADING FROM ENTRANCE HALL:

183 WILLIAM EDWARDS MILLER (active 1872–1909)
Lady Marjorie Erskine (1898–1967), 1908
The elder daughter of the 4th Marquess. Miller painted most of the figure from her sister, Lady Phyllis, who was sitting to him at the same time and enjoyed the experience more.

212 CLEMENT BURLISON (1815–99)
Theodora Wythes, Marchioness of Bristol
(1875–1957), as a Girl, 1886
The granddaughter and heiress of the great Victorian railway contractor George Wythes, she married the 4th Marquess in 1896. Her fortune paid not only for A.C.Blomfield's improvements to Ickworth in 1909–11, but also for the endowment which allowed the transfer of the estate to the National Trust in 1956.

185 WILLIAM EDWARDS MILLER (active 1872–1909)
Lady Phyllis MacRae (1899–1989), 1908
The younger daughter of the 4th Marquess.

WALL LEADING TO LIBRARY:

72 Sir ARTHUR COPE, RA (1857–1940)
Frederick William John, 3rd Marquess of Bristol
(1834–1907), 1905
The eldest son of the 2nd Marquess, he succeeded to the title in 1864. He commissioned the architect F.C.Penrose to make various improvements to Ickworth, including the magnificent Pompeian Room.

The gilt side-table ornamented with lion's heads was
probably supplied by Banting, France & Co. in 1829

329 REGINALD GRENVILLE EVES, RA (1876–1941)
Theodora Wythes, Marchioness of Bristol
(1875–1957), 1915

179 Sir ARTHUR COPE, RA (1857–1940)
Frederick William, 4th Marquess of Bristol
(1863–1951), 1908
Succeeded his uncle, the 3rd Marquess, in 1907. Seen here as a Captain in the Royal Navy, he rose to the rank of Rear-Admiral. His medals are displayed in the showcase below.

SCULPTURE

ON MANTELPIECE:

ELIZABETH BOUGHTON, LADY TEMPLETOWN (1747–1823)
The 1st Marquess of Bristol as a young man
Modelled by the sitter's mother-in-law, who was a talented amateur sculptor.

LORENZO BARTOLINI (1777–1850)
Elizabeth Albana, Marchioness of Bristol; carved in Florence *c*.1817–18, during the family's prolonged European tour (1817–21). The daughter of the previous sculptor.

ON GILT TABLE NEAR ENTRANCE:

CHRISTOPHER HEWETSON (1735–99)
The Earl-Bishop; carved in Rome *c*.1770.

FURNITURE

IN CENTRE OF ROOM:

The mahogany dining-table and set of twelve chairs were probably supplied to the 1st Marquess for 6 St James's Square by Banting, France & Co. in 1821.

ENTRANCE WALL:

The massive gilt side-table with granite top and the pair of gilt candlestands, ornamented with lion's heads, are thought to have been supplied by Banting, France & Co. in 1829.

FIREPLACE WALL:

The pair of French Empire tables with circular granite tops and tripod supports is in the style of Pierre-Antoine Bellangé, an *ébéniste* much patronised by Napoleon.

ON MANTELPIECE:

The French bronze and brass clock, set in white marble, has a movement by Jerclif of Paris, while the bronze figure of a negress above is signed 'Cordier, 1861'.

WINDOW WALL:

The pair of mid-18th-century Italian gilt Rococo pier-glasses and tables is thought to have been purchased by the 2nd Earl when Minister in Turin (1755–8).

CERAMICS

ON SIDE-TABLES:

A selection of pieces from the large Chinese export armorial dinner service, Qianlong, *c.*1780. Commissioned by the banker Robert Drummond to celebrate the marriage of his sister Elizabeth to John Augustus, Lord Hervey, in 1779, and showing the arms of Hervey impaling Drummond. Bought by the 3rd Marquess at the sale of John and Elizabeth's grandson, the 6th Lord Howard de Walden.

SILVER AND METALWORK

ON DINING-TABLE:

The four Rococo candelabra by Simon le Sage, 1758, form part of a set of twelve candelabra commissioned by the 2nd Earl for his embassy to Madrid (1758–61), and bear the crest of George II.

ON TABLES FLANKING CHIMNEYPIECE:

The two massive candelabra were given to the 1st Marquess in 1826 and 1840 by his tenants, as a gesture of thanks for not raising their rents during periods of agricultural depression.

ON TABLE IN FRONT OF WINDOW:

The ormolu table-centre with mirror base, French Empire in the style of Pierre-Philippe Thomire, is surmounted by an early 19th-century ormolu fruit stand.

The Library

The 19th-century 30-light glass chandelier was supplied by Perry & Co. for the Bristols' London house. It was damaged when the house was bombed during the Second World War, and remodelled from the remaining pieces.

THE LIBRARY

The great semicircular Library is the largest of the state rooms in the Rotunda, and represents a combination of the tastes of the 1st and 4th Marquesses. John Field's austere scheme of simple plasterwork and giant scagliola columns (supplied by the Coade factory at a cost of £332) was furnished by Banting, France & Co. in 1829 with four huge fitted rosewood bookcases and the 'capital Axminster Carpet'. The original curtains and upholstery were replaced in 1909–11 by the 4th Marquess, who moved the ornate carved and gilded pelmet boards from the Drawing Room to the Library, and commissioned the magnificent green and silver damask from the Gainsborough Silk Weaving Company.

Used occasionally in the 19th century for informal breakfasts, the Library doubled as a ballroom, notably for the annual servants' ball.

The acquisition of a number of key pictures at the 1996 sale of the contents of the East Wing was made possible with the generous support of the NACF and NHMF. A re-hang of the pictures in this and a number of other rooms followed.

CHIMNEYPIECE

The 'large Italian chimneypiece' fixed here by John Field in 1829 was almost certainly acquired in Rome by the Earl-Bishop. The pairs of figures flanking the fireplace are both versions of groups by Canova (Eros and Psyche to the left, Bacchus and Ariadne to the right), but are thought to be replicas by another Roman sculptor of the day, possibly a member of the Cardelli family.

PICTURES

FIREPLACE WALL:

49 After CLAUDE LORRAINE (1600–82)
Landscape with Two Figures dancing with Tambourines, known as 'The Mill'
The original is in the Doria-Pamphilj Gallery in Rome.

Prince Baltasar Carlos; by Velázquez, 1635 (Library)

DIEGO VELÁZQUEZ (1599–1660)
Prince Baltasar Carlos (1629–46) as a Hunter
The only and cherished son of Philip IV of Spain by his first marriage to Elizabeth of France. Painted in 1635, when he was six years old, with two greyhounds and a partridge-dog.

Attributed to BENEDETTO GENNARI (1633–1715)
The Hellespontic Sibyl
One of the twelve prophets who foretold the coming of Christ.

SPANISH SCHOOL, mid-17th-century
Portrait of a Boy with a Dog
Thought to have been acquired with the Velázquez (which it has always balanced at Ickworth) by the 1st Marquess during his Grand Tour of 1817–21.

BENJAMIN WEST, PRA (1738–1820)
The Death of Wolfe, 1779
General Wolfe died in 1759 on the Heights of Abraham in the battle which resulted in the capture of Quebec, and consequently of Canada, from the French. Wolfe was a friend of the Hervey family and an intimate of John, Lord Hervey's daughter, Lepel, Lady Mulgrave (1723–80). His ADC, Captain Hervey Smyth, shown to the left of the dying man, was a grandson of the 1st Earl. This, the fourth version of the painting, was done for the Earl-Bishop, who described Wolfe as: 'My military saint, who deserves much more to be canoniz'd than any religious one I have ever read of.'

SCULPTURE

BETWEEN DOORS TO LEFT AND RIGHT OF FIREPLACE:

After JOSEPH NOLLEKENS (1737–1823)
A set of four busts of leading British politicians, on yellow scagliola pedestals. From left to right: the 2nd Earl of Liverpool (1770–1828), Prime Minister, 1812–27, and brother-in-law of the 1st Marquess; George Canning (1770–1827), Prime Minister, 1827; Charles James Fox (1749–1806), a leader of the Whig party; William Pitt the Younger (1759–1806), Prime Minister, 1783–1801, 1804–6.

WINDOW WALL:

LORENZO BARTOLINI (1770–1850)
A bust of Lady Augusta Hervey, later Seymour (1798–1880), daughter of the 1st Marquess, carved in Florence, c.1817–18.

ELIZABETH BOUGHTON, LADY TEMPLETOWN (1747–1823)
A bust of Lady Augusta Hervey as a child, modelled by her grandmother, around the same time as the bust of her father in the Dining Room.

BOOKS

Expensively rebound for Theodora, Marchioness of Bristol in the early 1900s, the library is in fact the accumulation of many generations of Herveys. The oldest books now at Ickworth belonged to Sir William Hervey (1585–1660), and his eldest son, John (1616–79), a prominent figure at the court of Charles II. The collection is particularly rich in 18th-century books, including a rare series of political periodicals and many volumes with elaborate plates, collected by the 1st Earl. Other notable

contributors were Mary Lepel, the literary wife of John, Lord Hervey, and the 1st Marquess.

FURNITURE

BETWEEN DOORS TO LEFT AND RIGHT OF FIREPLACE:

The pair of Louis XV gilt side-tables with Russian malachite tops is said to have been presented to the 3rd Earl by Catherine the Great of Russia.

ON MANTELPIECE:

A 19th-century French clock by Le Dure of Paris, with figure of Diana the Huntress.

FLANKING FIREPLACE:

A pair of late 17th-century mirrors with gilt repoussé borders, one with cresting in the form of a viscount's coronet.

Two Louis XIV Boulle writing-tables in red tortoiseshell and brass (left of fireplace) and ebony and brass (right). Probably acquired by the 1st Marquess through the dealer E. H. Baldock.

The pair of gilt torchères carved with eagle's heads as supports is English, late 18th-century.

CENTRE OF ROOM:

The suite of rosewood settees with brass inlay came from 6 St James's Square, and is thought to have been supplied by Banting, France & Co. in 1821.

A rosewood chess- and backgammon-table with lyre supports, the set of twelve single rosewood chairs and the pair of rosewood writing-tables were probably supplied for the house by Banting, France & Co. in 1829.

The rosewood grand piano inlaid with brass is by Clementi, c.1820.

BETWEEN WINDOWS:

The pair of early 19th-century Portuguese gilt pier-glasses and tables is inset with landscapes after Vernet.

CENTRAL WINDOW BAY:

The pair of laburnum wood card-tables is English, c.1715.

CHANDELIER

The early 20th-century 36-light glass chandelier and six glass wall-sconces were installed by F. C. Osler & Co. in 1910.

The Death of Wolfe;
by Benjamin West,
1779 (Library)

CERAMICS

LEFT OF FIREPLACE:

A porcelain hawk, Qianlong, *c.*1780, and *a Doccia bowl in the form of a shell*, Florence, *c.*1760.

ON MANTELPIECE:

A pair of three-tiered stands from the dessert service supplied to the 1st Marquess by Jean-Pierre Feuillet of Paris about 1820.

RIGHT OF FIREPLACE:

A Doccia bowl in the form of a shell, Florence, *c.*1760, and *a Sèvres vase* with ormolu handles, *c.*1815.

THE DRAWING ROOM

The Drawing Room was extensively remodelled for the 4th Marquess and Marchioness by A. C. Blomfield in 1909–11. Blomfield introduced the deep moulded panels on the walls, the pedimented doorcases, and plain semicircular pelmet boards. He also recommended the gilding of John Field's simple plaster ceiling, and may have suggested the striking colour scheme of blue walls and rose silk upholstery, supplied once again by the Gainsborough Silk Weaving Company of Sudbury.

CHIMNEYPIECE

The marble chimneypiece with oval insets of different coloured marbles and micro-mosaic panels was installed by John Field in 1829, and may also have been one of the Earl-Bishop's acquisitions in Rome which reached Ickworth after his death.

PICTURES

FIREPLACE WALL:

ELISABETH VIGÉE-LEBRUN (1755–1842)
Frederick, 4th Earl of Bristol and Bishop of Derry (1730–1803), 1790
Painted at Naples and including a view of Vesuvius, which Mme Vigée-Lebrun claimed that he climbed every day.

124 GEORGE ROMNEY (1734–1802)
Lady Louisa Hervey, Countess of Liverpool (1770–1821)
The youngest daughter of the Earl-Bishop, she was brought up in virtual seclusion at Ickworth by her doting mother, who commissioned this portrait in 1793, two years before Louisa's marriage to the future 2nd Earl of Liverpool.

93 THOMAS GAINSBOROUGH, RA (1727–88)
John Augustus, Lord Hervey (1757–96)
The elder son of the Earl-Bishop. Probably painted

The Drawing Room

soon after his return from the War of American
Independence in 1783, in the uniform of a naval
Captain, with his dog Twitchet (named after his
admiral). He had a colourful private life and was
sacked as Ambassador to Florence in 1793. He died
at sea before his father and so never inherited
Ickworth.

WALL LEADING FROM LIBRARY:

13 ANGELICA KAUFFMAN, RA (1741–1807)
Lady Elizabeth Foster (1759–1824), 1786
The favourite daughter of the Earl-Bishop. Her
first marriage to an Irish MP, John Thomas Foster,
ended in disaster. She lived in a *ménage à trois* with
the 5th Duke and Duchess of Devonshire, and, after
the Duchess's death, married him, in 1809.

FAR WALL LEADING TO HALL:

44 THOMAS GAINSBOROUGH, RA (1727–88)
*Commodore the Hon. Augustus Hervey, later 3rd Earl
of Bristol* (1724–79), 1767
The second son of John, Lord Hervey, he pursued a
successful naval career and an amorous private life.
This portrait shows him as a Captain at the siege of
Moro Castle in 1762, with Havana in the background, and the ensign of the defeated Spanish
navy at his feet. Hervey rose to become a Lord of
the Admiralty (1771–5) and Vice-Admiral of the
Blue (1778). He succeeded as 3rd Earl in 1775.

ON TOP OF LOW BOOKCASE:

46 THOMAS GAINSBOROUGH, RA (1727–88)
Augustus Hervey (c.1765–82)
Octagonal. Oil on tin
The 3rd Earl's natural son by Kitty Hunter, the
daughter of a Lord of the Admiralty. Augustus was

killed in action while serving as a midshipman on *Le Courageux*, commanded by his cousin, Lord Mulgrave, at the relief of Gibraltar in October 1782. The unusual tin support suggests the picture was made to take to sea.

SCULPTURE

WINDOW WALL:

A pair of busts of the 2nd Marquess (1800–64) as a small boy in marble and plaster, possibly by Lady Templetown.

FURNITURE

TO LEFT OF DOOR FROM LIBRARY:

The gilt armchair with a semicircular back is one of a set of six in the room. They are thought to be Italian, late 18th-century, and were inherited by Theodora, Marchioness of Bristol from her family home, Copped Hall, Essex.

The Louis XVI upright parquetry secretaire is stamped Pierre Migeon, c.1770.

Lady Elizabeth Foster; by Angelica Kauffman, 1786 (Drawing Room)

FIREPLACE WALL:

The Louis XVI upright secretaire is decorated with military and musical trophies in marquetry.

The Régence (c.1710–30) kingwood serpentine-fronted commode with ormolu mounts is stamped H.F.

Louis XV marquetry serpentine-fronted commode with ormolu mounts.

CENTRE OF ROOM:

The circular centre-table on a tripod base decorated with floral marquetry on a walnut ground is thought to have been supplied to the 1st Marquess by Baldock, and forms one of a group of similar marquetry tables based on designs published by R. H. Bridgens in 1828.

The set of four rosewood upholstered armchairs was probably supplied by Banting, France & Co. in 1829.

The chess table has a top decorated with pictures of Roman ruins after Piranesi in pen and ink. The reeded column stem and base were supplied by a local furniture maker, J. G. Bullon of Bury St Edmunds, in 1833.

The charming Louis XVI marquetry woman's writing-desk is by Pierre Roussel (*maître ébéniste* in 1760).

The small Louis XVI parquetry table is by P. H. Mewesen (*maître ébéniste* in 1766).

WINDOW WALL:

The pair of early 19th-century Portuguese gilt pier-tables and glasses is inset with scenes after Vernet.

FAR WALL:

The low rosewood bookcase with marble and mosaic top was probably supplied by Banting, France & Co. in 1829.

The Empire clock with figures representing Artemis between Orestes and Iphigenia has a mid-18th-century movement by J. B. Baillon of Paris.

CERAMICS AND GLASS

LEFT OF DOOR FROM LIBRARY:

The two chestnut baskets are part of the Qianlong armorial service shown in the Dining Room.

LEFT OF CHIMNEYPIECE:

The Meissen coffee cup and saucer, c.1850–60, are decorated with the Hervey arms and are thought to

The early 19th-century Portuguese gilt pier-table and pier-glass in the Drawing Room

be trial pieces for a new armorial service which was never commissioned.

The ice pails, jug and basin are part of a large dessert service supplied to the 1st Marquess by Jean-Pierre Feuillet of Paris, *c*.1820.

RIGHT OF CHIMNEYPIECE:

The pair of Sèvres vases bearing portraits of King Louis-Philippe and Queen Amelie of France was presented to the 1st Marquess in 1850, when the deposed King and Queen were staying in Bury St Edmunds after the 1848 revolution.

FAR WALL:

Pair of 18th-century blue and gold Bohemian glass vases.

CHANDELIER

The early 19th-century glass chandelier was installed by the 1st Marquess, and electrified by F.C. Osler & Co. in 1910.

CARPET

The 'capital Axminster carpet' was supplied for the room by Banting, France & Co. in 1829.

THE EAST CORRIDOR ANTE-ROOM

PICTURE

LEFT OF CHINA CABINET:

225 POMPEO BATONI (1708–87)
Sir Robert Davers, 5th Bt (1729–63)
The brother-in-law of the Earl-Bishop, who had married his sister Elizabeth in 1752. Painted in Rome in 1756 during his Grand Tour. He later travelled to the Americas, and was killed by native Americans near Lake Huron in 1763.

Sir Robert Davers, 5th Bt; by Pompeo Batoni, 1756 (East Corridor Ante-Room)

CERAMICS

The large Edwardian fitted cabinet contains some of the best porcelain in the collection. This includes a gold and white chinoiserie service made at Meissen about 1730, more pieces from the Chinese export service bearing the arms of John Augustus, Lord Hervey and Elizabeth Drummond, and a magnificent mid-18th-century Doccia table-centre, purchased by the 3rd Marquess in 1868.

FURNITURE

The rosewood x-frame cane-seated chairs were supplied by Holland & Son to the 1st Marquess.

THE NEAR EAST CORRIDOR

This corridor formed the main link between the family wing to the east, and the Rotunda, whose huge rooms were brought into use only for entertaining. The simple vaulted plasterwork interiors have changed little since they were constructed for the 1st Marquess by John Field in 1826–7, and furnished with fitted mahogany bookcases by Banting, France & Co.

PICTURES

BOOKCASE WALL, CENTRE:

97 ALLAN RAMSAY (1713–84)
Mary Lepel, Lady Hervey (1696–1768)
Molly Lepel married John, Lord Hervey in 1720 and was a famous beauty and wit at the court of George II in her youth. This portrait shows her in old age, when she had retired to live with her father-in-law at 'sweet Ickworth'.

LEFT OF FIRST WINDOW:

60 ENGLISH SCHOOL, 1564
Francis Hervey (1534–1601/2)
The earliest authentic family portrait at Ickworth. He was a younger son of John Hervey of Ickworth (1490–1556), and is shown at the age of 30 wearing his chain of office as a Gentleman Pensioner to Queen Elizabeth.

RIGHT OF SECOND WINDOW:

109 ANGLO–DUTCH SCHOOL, *c.*1620/30
Sir William Hervey (1585–1660)
Knighted in 1608 by James I and MP for Bury St Edmunds in 1628. He inherited Ickworth in 1630

and raised a regiment to support the King, when the Civil War broke out in 1642. Grandfather of the 1st Earl.

ABOVE DOOR TO SMOKING ROOM:

87 JEAN-BAPTISTE VAN LOO (1684–1745)
John, 1st Earl of Bristol (1665–1751)
Commissioned by his son and painted in 1742, when he was 76. For biography, see p. 9.

FURNITURE

The mahogany cane-seated chairs are in the 'Chinese Chippendale' style, *c.*1760.

THE SMOKING ROOM

The Smoking Room gained its present name only around 1907, when the 4th Marquess decided that gentlemen guests and their cigars should be banished from the East Wing, and made to use what was then known as the Corridor Room. The room was redecorated in 1998 to reflect the original intentions of the 1st Marquess, who envisaged a richly furnished room of passage, serving as an introduction to the splendours to come in the Rotunda. The wallpaper was copied from an early 19th-century patented paper at the Public Record Office, and the carpet rewoven using fragments of the original found in a first-floor bedroom.

PICTURES

FIREPLACE WALL, LEFT OF FIREPLACE, BOTTOM ROW:

115 WILLIAM HOGARTH (1697–1764)
The Hervey Conversation-piece
John, Lord Hervey is in the centre, wearing a grey coat and holding his key as Vice-Chamberlain of the King's Household, and is surrounded by a group of his Whig friends. Some – like Hogarth – were also Freemasons. Next to him – presenting an architectural plan – the Surveyor of the King's Works, Henry Fox (1705–74), created Lord Holland in 1763. Further left, seated at a table – his brother, Stephen Fox (1704–76), created Earl of Ilchester in 1756. Precariously balanced on a chair is the leading Freemason, the Rev. John Theophilus Desaguliers (1683–1744), who had written a scientific treatise on balance. With his telescope he

The Smoking Room

looks towards a church, which probably provided a prosperous living. At the right are Henry Fox's great friend, the 3rd Duke of Marlborough (1706–58), wearing a red coat, and Hervey's intimate, Thomas Winnington (1696–1746), Paymaster-General in 1743. In the background is a statue of Minerva.

OVER FIREPLACE:

WILLIAM HOARE, RA (1707–92)
The future Earl-Bishop presenting his son John Augustus, later Lord Hervey, to William Pitt, Earl of Chatham, 1771
In 1770 Chatham, a former Prime Minister, made a powerful speech insisting on the importance of British naval power. John Augustus was about to embark on a naval career, and this picture seems to represent a kind of secular blessing by the object of his father's admiration.

RIGHT OF FIREPLACE, BOTTOM ROW:

116 HUBERT-FRANÇOIS GRAVELOT (1699–1773), JEAN-ETIENNE LIOTARD (1702–89) and others
Captain Augustus Hervey greeted by his Family
The future 3rd Earl, with his mother (seated on the left), his two married sisters, and their husbands, Constantine Phipps, later Lord Mulgrave, and George Fitzgerald. Thought to have been commissioned in October 1750, when all the sitters were in Paris, from Gravelot (for the ensemble) and Liotard (for the heads). In the event, Liotard completed only the heads of the Phippses, and Gravelot those of the Fitzgeralds and Lady Hervey. Lady Hervey was dissatisfied with the result, and subsequently had her own head and that of her son painted by some unknown artist back in England. The ship in the background seems to be the 3rd Earl's last command, the *Dragon*.

WALL ADJOINING NEAR EAST CORRIDOR,
BOTTOM ROW:

GASPARD POUSSIN (DUGHET) (1615–75)
A Classical Landscape
Painted by the brother–in–law of Nicolas Poussin.
His work became extremely popular in the 18th
century, when it helped to form the aesthetic of the
landscape garden. This painting was in the collection of John, Lord Hervey by 1741.

166 TITIAN (*c.*1487–1576)
Head of an Unknown Man
The nobility and intensity of the face in this
damaged early work by Titian make it the most
remarkable of the portraits in the collection.

WALL ADJOINING FAR EAST CORRIDOR, BOTTOM
ROW:

129 ELISABETH VIGÉE-LEBRUN (1755–1842)
Portrait of the Artist, 1791
Commissioned by the Earl-Bishop. The face is that
of her adored, but unsatisfactory daughter, Julie.

168 JACOPO AMIGONI (mid-1680s–1752)
Princess Caroline (1713–57)
The third daughter of George II. According to
Horace Walpole, 'she had conceived an unalterable
passion for [John] Lord Hervey, constantly marked
afterwards by all kind and generous offices to his
children'.

*Captain Augustus Hervey (later 3rd Earl of Bristol) greeted by his Family; by Gravelot, Liotard and others
(Smoking Room)*

*Self-portrait; by Elisabeth Vigée-Lebrun, 1791
(Smoking Room)*

SCULPTURE

LEFT OF CHIMNEYPIECE:

The bronze figure of Europa on the bull is derived from a model by Giambologna (1529–1608).

RIGHT OF CHIMNEYPIECE:

The bronze Cupid flying by a tree-stump appears to be 18th-century Italian or Flemish.

FURNITURE

FLANKING CHIMNEYPIECE:

The pair of mahogany tea-urn stands, with latticed galleries and feet in the shape of a horse's hoofs, is English, *c*.1755.

Two kingwood commodes, elaborately mounted with ormolu, in the Louis XV style.

The pair of unusual mahogany candlestands with carved latticework decoration is English, *c*.1760.

ON MANTELPIECE:

An ormolu clock in the form of a cupid and cornucopia, by Leracher, Paris.

WINDOW WALL:

The pair of gilt Rococo pier-glasses is in the style of John Vardy, carved with the Prince of Wales's feathers in the cresting, and possibly acquired by John, Lord Hervey as a perk of his office as Vice-Chamberlain of the Royal Household.

FAR WALL:

The unusual English serpentine-fronted commode veneered with imported Coromandel lacquer is in the French style, *c*.1760.

CERAMICS

NEAR AND FAR WALLS:

The pair of Chinese blue-and-white Dragoon jars and covers is Kangxi period (1666–1722). So-called because Augustus the Strong of Saxony is reputed to have exchanged a regiment of dragoons for a set.

WINDOW WALLS AND CENTRE:

The set of three Japanese Imari dishes with floral decoration on white ground is early 18th-century.

ON MANTELPIECE:

The pair of Chinese blue-and-white double gourd vases is late Ming, *c*.1640.

THE FAR EAST CORRIDOR

PICTURES

BOOKCASE WALL, LEFT-HAND END:

105 ENGLISH SCHOOL, late 17th-century
Sir Thomas Hervey (1625–94)
The third son of Sir William Hervey of Ickworth, he was knighted by Charles II for supporting the Royalist cause. He married Isabella May, the daughter of Sir Humphrey May, Vice-Chamberlain of King Charles II's household, and was the father of the 1st Earl. It may be the portrait by Henry Paert (active 1679–*c*.1699) mentioned in the 1st Earl's diary.

WINDOW WALL:

Attributed to JOHANN ZOFFANY (1733–1810)
The Children of John, Lord Hervey and Molly Lepel:
49 *Lady Caroline Hervey* (1736–1819)

140 *Lady Lepel Hervey, Lady Mulgrave* (1723–80)

114 *Colonel (later General) William Hervey, MP* (1732–1815)

62 *Frederick Augustus Hervey, 4th Earl of Bristol and Bishop of Derry* (1730–1803)

57 *Lady Emily Caroline Nassau Hervey* (1734–1814)

33 *Lady Mary Hervey, Mrs Fitzgerald* (1726–1815)

ON STAND:

Attributed to BARTOLOMEO DI GIOVANNI (active 1486–after 1493)
The Virgin and Child
The ornate late 19th-century frame suggests that it was a late acquisition for Ickworth.

FURNITURE

WINDOW WALL:

The set of four mahogany armchairs with cane seats and the pair of rosewood card-tables were probably supplied by Banting, France & Co. in 1829.

FAR WALL:

The 18th-century Flemish stamped-leather screen is unusually high.

THE WEST CORRIDOR AND ANTE-ROOMS

Although the exterior of the West Corridor was completed for the 1st Marquess in the mid-1830s, the interior was left unfinished until 1879, when the 3rd Marquess employed the architect Francis Cranmer Penrose and the fashionable decorator John Diblee Crace to carry out the present scheme of stencilled and lined decoration. This was painted over during the Edwardian period, and re-created in 1995, using over 26 different colours.

SCULPTURE

B. F. HARDENBERG (active 1800–23)
The 2nd Earl of Liverpool (1770–1828), brother-in-law of the 1st Marquess, and Prime Minister, 1812–27

JOSEPH NOLLEKENS (1737–1823)
William Pitt the Younger (1759–1806), Prime Minister, 1783–1801, 1804–6

WILLIAM BEHNES (1795–1864)
The 1st Marquess of Bristol (1769–1859), 1833

The porphyry scagliola columns were supplied by Banting, France & Co. in 1829.

The West Corridor

THE POMPEIAN ROOM

Like the West Corridor, this room was not completed until 1879, when the 3rd Marquess employed Penrose and Crace to carry out the present scheme.

The grandson of Frederick Crace, who worked for George IV at Brighton Pavilion and at Windsor, and the son of John Gregory Crace, chosen by Charles Barry to decorate the Houses of Parliament, John Dibblee Crace was famous for his Italian Renaissance style of painted decoration, notably in the Library at Longleat in Wiltshire, and on the staircase of the National Gallery in London.

Penrose suggested that Crace should base his designs on the Roman wall-paintings uncovered in 1777 at the Villa Negroni on the Esquiline Hill in Rome. These had a special connection with the Bristol family: the figure panels from the original frescoes were actually purchased by the Earl-Bishop, who was in Italy at the time of their discovery. A set of proof engravings of the frescoes, dedicated to the Earl-Bishop, has been preserved at Ickworth, and would have been used by Crace as a reference source. The figure painting was carried out by Henry Scholz, one of the Crace firm's senior artists.

The decoration of the Pompeian Room was based on Roman wall-paintings discovered in the Villa Negroni in 1777

SCULPTURE

FIREPLACE WALL, ABOVE BOOKCASES:

SABATINO DE ANGELIS & FILS
A pair of bronze figures of wrestlers, stamped Naples, 1900. After the Antique.

WINDOW WALL:

Charles Rose Ellis, Lord Seaford (1771–1845), husband of Elizabeth Hervey, only child of John Augustus, Lord Hervey.

The 2nd Earl of Liverpool (1770–1828), after Sir Francis Chantrey (1781–1841).

FAR WALL:

SABATINO DE ANGELIS & FILS
Narcissus, bronze, stamped Naples, 1900.

FURNITURE

FIREPLACE WALL:

The fitted ebony bookcases were designed for the room by Crace.

The bronze and gilt clock with a figure of Father Time is by Charles Frodsham, Paris, *c.*1880.

WINDOW WALL:

The pair of oak pier-tables with inlaid marble tops is English, 18th-century.

CENTRE OF ROOM:

The centre-table, with inlaid specimen marbles, is Roman, mid-18th-century. The central micro-mosaic scene of doves drinking from a bowl derives from a model discovered at Hadrian's villa in 1737.

(Opposite page) The Pompeian Room

Return to the Entrance Hall and climb the stairs.

FURNITURE

ON HALF-LANDING:

A marquetry secretaire, designed by George Jack and made by Morris & Co. in 1906. On loan from the Hon. David Erskine.

SCULPTURE

Boy and Dolphin, by Joseph Nollekens (1737–1823). The subject is taken from Aelian's *On the Characteristics of Animals*, in which a tame dolphin accidentally causes the death of a boy, and then drowns itself in remorse. Originally bought by the Earl-Bishop for Downhill (see p. 45), believing it to be by Raphael.

THE MUSEUM LANDING

Remodelled by Blomfield in 1909–11, the landing was once used to display a collection of architectural models and souvenirs from the family's travels. Only one model, that of Ickworth itself, now remains, and the landing is used to show part of the remarkable collection of fans acquired by Geraldine, Marchioness of Bristol. Her portrait, which shows her holding one of the finest fans in the collection, stands on an easel at the rear of the landing.

PICTURES

FIREPLACE WALL:

307 After ALBRECHT DÜRER (1471–1528)
Self-portrait at the age of 28
The greatest artist of the German Renaissance. Derived from his self-portrait in the guise of Christ, now in the Alte Pinakothek, Munich. First recorded in the 1st Earl's London house in 1721. The Earl-Bishop was to show a particular interest in Dürer, planning to hang paintings of the German School in one of the wings at Ickworth.

After GUERCINO (1591–1666)
Jacob blessing Ephraim and Manasseh
Near to death, Jacob blesses his grandsons, but in doing so, crosses his hands, which cancels the blessing, to his son Joseph's alarm. The crossed hands were seen as a prophesy of Christ's cross.

(Right) The Upper Staircase Hall

321 After HANS HOLBEIN the Younger (1497/8–1543)
Sir Nicholas Poyntz (1510–57)
A prominent courtier under Henry VIII, and connection by marriage of William, Lord Hervey of Kidbrooke, whose daughter Elizabeth married John Hervey of Ickworth, the 1st Earl's uncle. The picture is first recorded in John, Lord Hervey's collection in 1741.

WALL OPPOSITE FIREPLACE:

JACOB MORE (1740–93)
Ideal Classical Landscape with Cicero, his Villa and Friends, 1780
The only known survivor of at least fourteen pictures painted for the Earl-Bishop by the 'Scottish

Ideal Classical Landscape with Cicero, his Villa and Friends; by Jacob More, 1780 (Museum Landing)

Claude', who acted for him not only as an artist, but also as a dealer, agent and informant in Rome. Acquired from the 7th Marquess in 1993, with generous help from the NACF.

ON EASEL:

The Hon. HENRY GRAVES (1818–82)
Geraldine Anson, Marchioness of Bristol (1843–1927), 1870
Shown holding one of the best examples from her important collection of fans, part of which is displayed on the Museum Landing.

LEFT-HAND LANDING ABOVE STAIRCASE:

37 Manner of Sir ANTHONY VAN DYCK (1599–1641)
The Hon. Elizabeth Hervey of Kidbrooke, Mrs John Hervey (c.1615–1700)
Heiress of Lord Hervey of Kidbrooke, she married her cousin John Hervey. On her husband's death in 1679, she inherited the Ickworth estates and the ancient Hervey manor house, but by the time she died it was in ruins, following a long dispute with her brother-in-law, Sir Thomas Hervey (d.1694).

SCULPTURE

HEAD OF STAIRCASE:

EDMÉ BOUCHARDON (1698–1762)
A terracotta bust of John, Lord Hervey (1696–1743), signed and dated Rome, 1729. It was modelled during Lord Hervey's Grand Tour of Italy in 1728–9. The marble versions were based on this (see p. 8).

CARLO MAROCHETTI (1805–67)
A marble bust of Eliza Seymour, Viscountess Clifden (d.1896), 1854. The daughter of Frederick and Lady Augusta Seymour (see p. 14).

MODEL

The wood and papier-mâché model of Ickworth was made in 1796 by the Rev. Joseph Sandys, the brother of the Earl-Bishop's architect. It is thought to have been constructed to send to the Earl-Bishop in Italy, so that he might have some idea of the progress on the house, and the Sandys brothers' interpretation of Asprucci's original designs. The Rotunda was built almost exactly as shown in the model, but the corridors and wings were redesigned by John Field for the 1st Marquess.

THE MUSEUM ROOM

The former East Bedroom was redecorated in 1995 to display the fine family collections of silver, miniatures and objects of virtu.

PICTURES

FIREPLACE WALL, TOP ROW:

DOMINIC SERRES (1722–93)
A group, originally of seven paintings, recording episodes in the naval career of Augustus Hervey, later 3rd Earl of Bristol (1724–79):

Captain Augustus Hervey in the 'Hampton Court' firing at the French frigate 'Nymph' off the coast of Majorca, 21 June 1758, 1769

Captain Augustus Hervey in the 'Phoenix' taking 14 French ships at Argenteira, 9 November 1756, 1769

BOTTOM ROW:

Commodore Augustus Hervey taking the Port La Trinité and the north side of the island of Martinique, 11 February 1762, 1766

A Naval Action, 1763
Lacks any identifying inscription, so may, like the next picture, not represent one of Captain Hervey's actions.

Lord Rodney in HMS 'Formidable' bringing in the 'Ville de Paris' and two other French warships into Port Royal, Jamaica, after the Battle of the Saints on 12 April 1782, 1788

ABOVE DOOR:

OZIAS HUMPHRY, RA (1742–1810) after THOMAS GAINSBOROUGH, RA (1727–88)
Commodore the Hon. Augustus Hervey, later 3rd Earl of Bristol (1724–79)
Copy of the portrait in the Drawing Room (no. 44) commissioned by Hervey's mistress, Mary Nesbitt, in 1788.

WINDOW WALL:

200 JOHANN ZOFFANY (1733–1810)
George William, 2nd Earl of Bristol (1721–75)
The eldest son of John, Lord Hervey. He inherited the Earldom on his grandfather's death in 1751. He was the British Envoy to Turin and Ambassador to Madrid (1758–61). In 1766 he was made Lord Lieutenant of Ireland and a Privy Counsellor. Like his father, he became Lord Privy Seal (1768–70),

and ended his career as Groom of the Stole and First Lord of the Bedchamber to George III.

FAR WALL:

ANTONIO DE BITTIO (1722–97)
Elizabeth Davers, Countess of Bristol (1730–1800), *with her youngest daughter, Lady Louisa Hervey* (1770–1821)
Elizabeth, daughter of Sir Jermyn Davers, 4th Bt, of Rushbrooke Hall, married the future 4th Earl in 1752. The couple separated in 1782 and Lady Bristol retired to live at Ickworth with her two youngest children, Frederick and Louisa. Louisa married the future 2nd Earl of Liverpool in 1795.

SILVER

The Bristol silver is outstanding both for its quality and quantity; few country houses retain such complete sets of 18th-century dining and dessert plate. It is shown in a set of unusual cases, designed for the National Trust in 1958 by the Suffolk architect Raymond Erith.

ENTRANCE WALL:

Case I contains early 18th-century pieces purchased by the 1st Earl. Many of these are by Huguenot makers working in London, such as Philip Rollos, Simon Pantin, Paul Crespin and Paul de Lamerie. The most notable piece is the magnificent Baroque wine cistern made in 1680 by Robert Cooper and

A tureen topped with the Hervey snow leopard; by Frederick Kandler, 1752 (Museum Room)

A wine cooler, by Philip Rollos, 1710 (Museum Room)

bought by the 1st Earl in 1697 from the executors of his uncle, Baptist May. Also on display in this case are pieces of church plate on loan from Ickworth and Horringer churches.

WINDOW WALL AND FAR WALL:

Cases II and III contain mid- to late 18th-century Rococo pieces bought by the 2nd Earl. Many bear the arms of George II and would have been supplied for diplomatic or official purposes: Lord Bristol was Minister at Turin (1755–8), Ambassador to Madrid (1758–61), and Lord Lieutenant of Ireland (1766–7). Government officials were provided with an allowance to buy plate, and Lord Bristol appears to have favoured two London silversmiths: Frederick Kandler and Simon Le Sage.

MINIATURES

The Ickworth collection of miniatures is one of the most outstanding private collections in Britain, surpassed only by those belonging to the Duke of Buccleugh and the late Earl Beauchamp at Madresfield. It is very much a family affair, begun by Sir Thomas Hervey (1625–94), and added to until Ickworth was handed over to the Trust in 1956. The most dedicated collectors of Hervey family portraits were the 1st Earl, his son Lord Hervey, and his grandson, the Earl-Bishop. More recently, Theodora, Marchioness of Bristol scoured auction catalogues and salerooms for miniatures with Hervey connections.

ENTRANCE WALL, BY WINDOW:

The tabletop display case contains 17th- and 18th-century miniatures, including a group of portraits of members of the British and Sardinian royal families. The early miniatures include examples by John Hoskins, Nicholas Dixon and Peter Cross, while the 18th century is represented by Bernard Lens, Samuel Cotes, Nathaniel Hone, Christian Zincke and John Smart.

FIREPLACE WALL:

The tabletop display case is devoted to miniatures of the Earl-Bishop and his descendants. These include pairs of miniatures by John Downman and Richard Cosway, enamels by Henry Bone and Joseph Lee, and individual examples by Richard Dighton, William Maw Egley, Mrs Mee and Sir William Ross.

OBJECTS OF VIRTU

FAR WALL:

The tabletop display case contains snuffboxes, jewelled watches, seals and scent bottles, mostly 18th-century, but of varying nationalities.

FIREPLACE WALL:

The Morris & Co. upright display case was made for Geraldine, Marchioness of Bristol to store and display her collection of fans. It is now used to show another of her collections – tiny jointed silver fish, used as scent bottles and vinaigrettes.

CERAMICS

The pair of candlestands in the form of cherubs is from the mid-18th-century Doccia table-centre purchased by the 3rd Marquess in 1868, and shown in the East Corridor Ante-Room.

THE BATHROOM

This oddly shaped and austere bathroom, with its high ceiling and tall window, was one of several installed in 1909–11 by Blomfield for the 4th Marquess. The mahogany washstand is also Edwardian.

THE WEST BEDROOM

As the Bristol family lived in the East Wing, the bedrooms in the Rotunda were intended solely for use by guests during large house parties or shooting weekends. Some were even left unfinished until the Edwardian period, and this is one of several rooms remodelled by Blomfield in 1909–11.

PICTURES

FIREPLACE WALL, LEFT OF FIREPLACE:

GEORGE KNAPTON (1698–1778) after Sir GODFREY KNELLER (1646/9–1723)
Molly Lepel, Lady Hervey (1696–1768), 1756
For biography, see p. 19.

RIGHT OF BED:

197 HUGH DOUGLAS HAMILTON (1736–1808)
The Earl-Bishop (1730–1803), before a vista of Rome, 1790
The Earl-Bishop is seated in a corner of the Borghese Gardens known as the Pincian Hill, looking down over Rome. The original designs for Ickworth were drawn up by Mario Asprucci, architect of many buildings, including the Villa Aesculapius, in the area of the Villa Borghese gardens designed by Jacob More and known as the 'Giardino Inglese'. Hamilton was an Irish artist who worked in Rome from 1782 to 1791. Acquired from the 7th Marquess in 1993, with the generous help of the NACF and NHMF.

WINDOW WALL:

73 ANTON RAPHAEL MENGS (1728–79)
George William, 2nd Earl of Bristol (1721–75)
For biography, see p. 28. This pastel is thought to have been done at the end of Lord Bristol's embassy to Madrid (1758–61).

RIGHT OF DOOR:

173 FRIEDRICH REHBERG (1758–1835)
Frederick William, Lord Jermyn (1800–64), 1818
The eldest son of the 1st Marquess, drawn in Rome on the Grand Tour, with the Capitol behind. He was MP for Bury St Edmunds (1826–59) and for West Suffolk (1859), and Treasurer of the Royal Household (1841–6). He succeeded as 2nd Marquess in 1859.

(Right) Molly Lepel, Lady Hervey; pastel by George Knapton after Sir Godfrey Kneller, 1756 (West Bedroom)

FRIEDRICH REHBERG (1758–1835)
Lord George Hervey (1803–38) and Lord William Hervey (1805–50), 1818
The second and the third sons of the 1st Marquess, drawn in Rome at the same time as their brother. The boys are examining their collection of Antique seals, a common souvenir of the Grand Tour.

FURNITURE

The massive mahogany bed was supplied to the 1st Marquess in 1829 by Banting, France & Co. The present bed-hangings were copied in 1986 by Baker & Co. from the chintz that was originally on the bed. They are lined in the same pink chintz which forms the backdrop to the bed; the roof of the tester is the original, as are all the tassels on the bed and curtains. The window curtains and pelmets were copied from originals found in the house.

The rosewood chaise-longue and the pair of mahogany chests-of-drawers with marble tops were also supplied by Banting, France & Co. in 1829.

CERAMICS

ON MANTELPIECE:

The three chestnut baskets are part of the Qianlong armorial service shown in the Dining Room.

BETWEEN WINDOWS:

The pair of candlestands is from the mid-18th-century Doccia table-centre shown in the East Corridor Ante-Room.

THE WEST DRESSING ROOM

Like the adjoining bedroom, this room was remodelled in 1909–11 by Blomfield for the 4th Marquess.

PICTURES

OPPOSITE FIREPLACE:

JOHN DOWNMAN, ARA (*c*.1750–1824)
Lady Mary Hervey, Countess of Erne (1753–1842)
with her daughter, Lady Elizabeth Creichton (d.1856), 1781
Lady Mary was the eldest daughter of the Earl-Bishop. In 1776 she married the future 1st Earl of Erne of Crom Castle in Co. Fermanagh. Their daughter Elizabeth married James Stuart Wortley, 1st Lord Wharncliffe in 1799.

Lady ELIZABETH FOSTER (1759–1824)
A Swiss Cottage near the Lake of Lausanne

A View of the Island of Capri from the Ruins of Pollio's Villa near Naples, 1795

WINDOW WALL:

40 Sir THOMAS LAWRENCE, PRA (1769–1830)
Cardinal Consalvi (1754–1824), 1819
Chamberlain and adviser to Pope Pius VII. He owed his position to the patronage of the Cardinal of York, the younger brother of Bonnie Prince Charlie. Cardinal Consalvi was a friend of Lady Elizabeth Foster, who acquired this drawing from Lawrence in Rome in 1819, when he came to paint the Pope and the Cardinal.

15 JOHN DOWNMAN, ARA (*c*.1750–1824)
Georgiana, Duchess of Devonshire (1757–1806) *and Lady Elizabeth Foster* (1759–1824), 1785
The Duchess of Devonshire, with her great friend and successor as Duchess, Lady Elizabeth Foster.

FURNITURE

The mahogany 'couch bedstead with scroll ends stuffed and chintz covered' was supplied by Banting, France & Co. in 1829. The chintz used for the bed and curtains is the original copied for the refurbishment of the West Bedroom.

The mirror-fronted bureau and marble-topped chest-of-drawers are also likely to have been supplied by Banting, France & Co.

CERAMICS

ON MANTELPIECE:

*A pair of Meissen vases, c.*1800, ornamented with '*Deutsche Blumen*' ('German flowers'). Part of an original set of eight.

THE BASEMENT

For the majority of the year the Bristol family lived and ate in the East Wing, while the household servants would have used the sizeable kitchens and service areas in the basement of the East Wing. A complete set of additional offices was also provided under the Rotunda, including kitchen, servants' hall, beer and wine cellars, housekeeper's and butler's rooms. Blomfield remodelled the kitchen and servants' hall in 1909–11 to provide better cooking ranges and heating equipment.

At present the kitchen and servants' hall are used as the shop and restaurant, though it is hoped that they will be restored to their former status in the future.

THE GARDEN AND PARK

THE GARDEN

Visitors to Ickworth have long remarked on the curious division between the 19th-century gardens surrounding the house and the much earlier walled garden near the church. The survival of two quite separate gardens reflects the 1st Earl's unfulfilled desire in the early 18th century for a family seat on the site of Ickworth Hall (see p. 49). Instead of creating a garden for his temporary home, Ickworth Lodge, he concentrated all his attention on forming a worthy setting for the proposed house. The gardens of the original Tudor manor, covering nearly ten acres of land sloping southward from the church, were gradually swept away; in their place the 1st Earl installed a formal garden, with a canal and summer-house (attributed to William Talman, c.1703), and a huge kitchen garden protected by high brick walls (c.1713). Lord Bristol's grandiose building plans were destined to remain unexecuted, and

three generations of Herveys were forced to contemplate a short carriage ride from Ickworth Lodge if they wished to take a stroll in the pleasure grounds.

This somewhat ridiculous situation finally came to an end in 1829, when the 1st Marquess moved into the recently completed East Wing. The long-awaited mansion had been built on a new site, halfway between the Lodge and the church, and its 180-metre façade offered challenging opportunities for landscaping. Family correspondence shows that Lord Bristol did not approach a professional garden designer, but relied instead on the advice of his enthusiastic great-nephew, Charles Ellis, 6th Lord Howard de Walden. Lord Howard de Walden responded to the distinctive classical design of the Rotunda and surrounded the southern front with an appropriately Italianate formal garden. Plantations of evergreens were edged with clipped box hedges,

The south front from the terraced walk

interspersed with walks of pencil cypresses. A long central path from the Rotunda leads, up a flight of steps, to a raised, gently curving terraced walk. The walk, over 120 metres long, is bounded by a low wall and provides wide views over the park and the site of Ickworth Hall.

If this type of garden was unusual for its date, prefiguring the later 19th-century fashion for semi-formal Italian gardening, the treatment of the entrance front was to be even more idiosyncratic. Instead of creating a grand vista, the 1st Marquess allowed the dense belt of oaks and cedars originally planted to hide the building works to grow to its full height. This 'Building Plantation' deliberately shielded all views of the house from the north, and gave visitors approaching from the main drive no hint of the surprise to come when they rounded the corner and found themselves confronted by the astonishing bulk of the Rotunda. To the west of the house, he adapted an existing section of orna-mental woodland (possibly laid out by Capability Brown in the 1770s as an adjunct to Ickworth Lodge) to create the Albana Walk. A pleasure-ground walk named in honour of his wife, Elizabeth Albana Upton, this leafy path provided an easy walking surface for ladies, bordered by clipped box hedges and ornamented with summer-houses and viewing points.

The last major element of the garden to be intro-duced was the Orangery with its adjoining terrace,

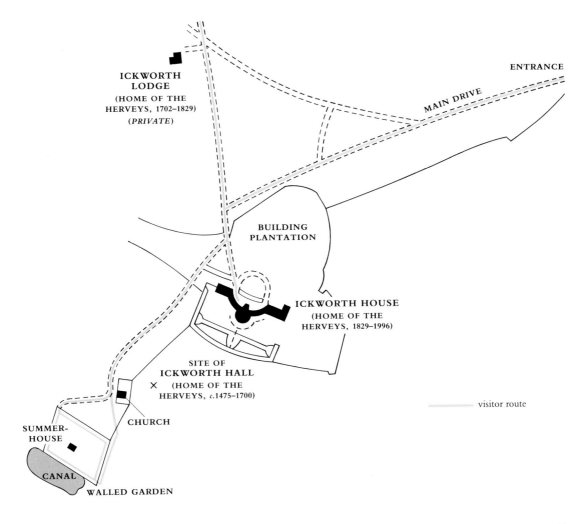

The 1st Earl's summer-house, with the church and the Rotunda beyond

added when the exterior of the West Wing was finally completed in 1841. The basic framework of the garden has changed little since that date, although later generations made minor improvements. The 3rd Marquess and Marchioness introduced formal flower-beds (since grassed over) to the South Garden, and replaced an ornamental shrubbery on the terrace below the entrance front with the present semicircular lawn. Emulating his grandfather, the 3rd Marquess also created a woodland path named after his wife – Lady Geraldine's Walk, running along the perimeter of the Building Plantation. Direct access from the Rotunda to the garden was provided only in 1912, when the 4th Marquess asked A.C. Blomfield to design a set of steps from a newly opened-up French window in the Library.

THE PARK

The 1st Earl may not have been able to realise his dream of a new family seat at Ickworth, but between 1700 and 1731 he created a park worthy of the Hervey name. As the original 13th-century deer-park had long since disappeared, Lord Bristol was forced to carve his new landscape out of a network of small fields. Tenants were removed from over 1,200 acres of surrounding land, and given new homes in Horringer village. Buildings were demolished and old agricultural boundaries grassed over, leaving an intriguing surface record for modern archaeologists. By 1706 deer could be reintroduced to the park, protected by new groves and plantations within a lengthy paling fence. Contemporaries were quick to appreciate Lord Bristol's achievement; Thomas Robinson described Ickworth in 1731 as 'by much the finest park I ever yet saw, being about 1,200 acres and above 25,000 pounds of exceeding fine timber', while an anonymous diarist of the 1750s discovered 'a large pleasant park ... full ten miles round finely situated in open fertile sporting country', 'extreamly well wooded', with 'several fine Country Views ... well stocked with cattle and sheep and deer ... in general in fine order'.

Further improvements were made between 1769 and 1776, when the 2nd Earl employed Capability Brown. Unfortunately Brown's account books do not describe the work done, but he probably concentrated on improving the approach to Ickworth Lodge, and on laying out the ornamental woodland which forms the bones of the present Albana Walk. The main drive from Horringer may well have been Brown's work, with its carefully framed views to and from the Lodge. More surprisingly, Brown also seems to have created vistas radiating from the proposed site for Ickworth House – perhaps anticipating the plans he drew up for the Earl-Bishop in 1781–2.

Whereas the 18th-century parkland had been designed to incorporate views of the surrounding countryside, the 19th-century owners of Ickworth sought to enclose the park within a dense belt of plantations. The 1st Marquess employed contract labour to create a series of new woods along the boundary, and to provide a setting for the Obelisk, erected in 1817 to the memory of the Earl-Bishop by the people of Derry. This planting regime was continued by the 3rd Marquess, ensuring that the house was screened from all directions, with only the very top of the Rotunda visible from distant roads. The Fairy Lake at the south-east corner of the park is also thought to have been created by the 3rd Marquess, and once contained an ornamental boat-house. His successor, the 4th Marquess, was an enthusiastic amateur tree surgeon, who frequently surprised visitors to the park by greeting them from the upper branches.

The Fairy Lake

ICKWORTH AND THE HERVEYS

EARLY HISTORY

When the Norman invaders made their Domesday survey in 1086, the manor of Ickworth was among the many possessions of the monks of nearby St Edmundsbury, then one of the most powerful abbeys in England. Ownership subsequently passed to a family who bore the name of de Ickworth from the mid-12th century. Sir Thomas de Ickworth was granted a licence by the Abbey to create a deer-park at Ickworth in 1253, and may have built the small 13th-century half-timbered hall found during excavations in 1986 near Ickworth church.

Ickworth remained in the ownership of this family until 1432, when the death of the last direct heir provoked a lengthy dispute. Among the most determined claimants to the manor was Abbot William Curteys, who believed that it should revert to St Edmundsbury, but Ickworth was eventually granted to Sir William Drury of Rougham, a descendant by marriage of the de Ickworths. Sir William promptly gave the estate to his cousin, Henry Drury, whose daughter Jane married Thomas Hervey, ancestor of the Herveys of Ickworth.

The family of Hervey, or Herve, was of French origin, and had held considerable property in East Anglia since the Norman Conquest. One branch settled in Bedfordshire after acquiring the manor of Thurleigh by marriage. Thomas Hervey, who was a younger son of a 15th-century owner of Thurleigh, made a similarly advantageous alliance when he married the heiress of Ickworth. Sadly neither he nor Jane were to enjoy the full fruits of their inheritance, as both were outlived by Jane's mother, Elizabeth Drury, who occupied Ickworth Hall as a tenant-for-life.

(Right) Sir Francis Hervey, 1564 (East Corridor)

THE TUDOR HERVEYS

Thomas and Jane's son, William Hervey of Ickworth (1464–1538), was the founder of a courtly dynasty who prospered throughout the Tudor period. While the eldest sons remained at Ickworth, busy converting the ancient hall of the de Ickworths into a modern brick manor house, the younger sons pursued successful careers at the courts of Henry VIII, Mary and Elizabeth.

Of William's three sons, John, Nicholas and Edmund, John as the eldest inherited Ickworth,

where he lived until his death in 1556. The two younger sons were introduced to court by their cousin, Sir George Hervey of Thurleigh, and were left to sink or swim. Nicholas, who took part in the famous jousts at the Field of the Cloth of Gold in 1520, quickly won the King's favour and rose to become a gentleman of the Privy Chamber. In 1530–1 Sir Nicholas (as he had then become) was appointed Ambassador to the court of Emperor Charles V, where he strongly supported his master's efforts to divorce Catherine of Aragon.

Although Sir Nicholas died young in 1532, his spectacular rise ensured places at court for the next generation. Once again the head of the family, William (1526–92), remained in Suffolk, marrying into an important local family, the Poleys of Boxted. William's younger brother, Francis (1534–1601/2), joined his cousins Sir Thomas and Henry to seek his fortune at the court of Queen Mary. Francis Hervey, who was swiftly appointed to the corps of Gentlemen Pensioners, became a close associate of Elizabeth's favourite, the Earl of Essex, and sat as an MP in five Elizabethan parliaments. His portrait, in which he wears the gold chain of the Gentleman Pensioner, is the earliest authentic image of a Hervey to remain in the Ickworth collection.

ICKWORTH UNDER THE STUARTS

Herveys continued to serve the Crown under the Stuarts. William Hervey (1585–1660), the eldest son of John Hervey of Ickworth, was knighted by James I in 1608, and served as a commissioner in 1618 for surveying Lincoln's Inn Fields. Court connections were reinforced by marriage: Sir William's brother-in-law, Thomas Jermyn, was a Privy Counsellor and Vice-Chamberlain to Charles I. A loyal royalist, William Hervey briefly joined Jermyn in the Commons as MP for Bury in the short-lived Parliament of 1628.

At the outbreak of the Civil War in 1642, Sir William raised a regiment in support of the King. Chivalry was quickly followed by romance. As a young man, he had courted the attractive Lady Penelope Rivers of neighbouring Hengrave Hall. Legend has it that when Sir George Trenchard, Sir

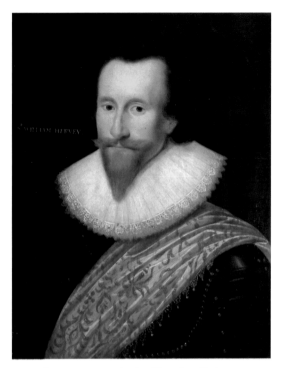

Sir William Hervey, c.1620/30 (East Corridor)

John Gage and Sir William Hervey all courted her at the same time, she told them that if they would only have patience, she would accept all of them in their turns. Lady Penelope was as good as her word; Sir John Gage died in 1642, and within the year she had married Sir William, whose first wife, Susan Jermyn, had died in 1637.

Sir William left Ickworth for Hengrave in 1642, and seems to have handed his property over to his eldest son John (1616–79), possibly in order to avoid sequestration by Parliament. Described by the historian Collins as 'a person of great worth and accomplishments' and a 'patron of learned men', John Hervey was a close friend of the courtier-soldier Robert Sidney, Earl of Leicester. Hervey travelled on the Continent in his youth, staying with Leicester while he was Ambassador in Paris in 1636–41, and thereafter lived largely in London. A royalist like his father, he successfully negotiated with Parliament to retain the Ickworth estate in 1655, but showed no interest in living in Ickworth Hall, which was let to a succession of tenants.

Elizabeth Hervey of Kidbrooke, who inherited Ickworth after the death of her husband, John Hervey, in 1679

Hervey's career took off after the Restoration in 1660. Nominated by the Crown as one of the MPs for the Cinque Ports, Hervey sat for Hythe in the Parliament of 1661–79. According to Bishop Burnet, he earned the respect of Charles II:

Upon a great occasion he voted against that which the King desired. So the King chid him for it. Next day another important question falling in, he voted as the King would have him. So the King took notice of it at night, and said 'You were not against me to-day'. He answered, 'No, sir, I was against my conscience today'. This was so gravely delivered that the King seemed pleased; and it was much talked of.

Hervey also enjoyed the patronage of his influential first cousin, Henry Jermyn, 1st Earl of St Albans. St Albans, who had been Chamberlain to Queen Henrietta Maria, may have recommended Hervey for the post of Treasurer to the new Queen, Catherine of Braganza. This position, although prominent, was a mixed blessing; Charles II's long-suffering Queen was frequently kept short of funds, and the Treasurer often had to dip into his own

pockets to pay outstanding bills. Hervey's role as trustee to the St Albans estate also enabled him in 1677 to acquire 6 St James's Square, the family's London home until 1955.

Ever pragmatic, Hervey expanded the family estates by marrying a cousin, the Hon. Elizabeth Hervey. Elizabeth was the only surviving child of Lord Hervey of Kidbrooke, a descendant of Sir Nicholas Hervey, Ambassador to Charles V in the reign of Henry VIII. Over 40 when she married, Elizabeth appears to have been something of a spoilt heiress, causing no end of trouble to her husband's family following his death in 1679. Although the majority of John Hervey's property, including the Ickworth estate, was left to her for life, Mrs Hervey repeatedly went to court to enforce further payments. John's nephew, the future 1st Earl of Bristol, wrote despairingly to Sir Charles Holt in 1695: 'I should have addressed myself to you sooner, but there having happened great controversies between my said aunt and father, touching my said uncle's estate, and several transactions between her and me since my father's death, we have had our hands and heads too full of that suit to mind other matters.'

THE 1ST EARL OF BRISTOL (1665–1751)

John Hervey, 1st Earl of Bristol was the first Hervey to live at Ickworth for nearly 60 years. The intransigent Mrs Hervey lived on until 1700, and John's parents, Sir Thomas and Lady Isabella Hervey, had made their home in Bury. Thomas and Isabella were an exceptionally loving couple, whose romantic history became a family legend. Isabella's father, Sir Humphrey May, strongly opposed her marriage to a younger son, and kept the lovers apart for over ten years. The affectionate letters written during this period were preserved by their children, along with the poems composed each year by the grieving Sir Thomas on the anniversary of his wife's death. The first, written in 1687, is among the most heartfelt:

Lord bring me to that bliss
In which I hope she is;
And there together let us ever shine,
Where I nor her's shall be, nor she be mine,
But may again be joined in being Thine.

Their son John Hervey's grief at the death of his first wife, Isabella Carr, was to be equally intense. Heiress to large estates at Aswarby in Lincolnshire, Isabella died during childbirth in 1693. Two years later, the reluctant widower was seeking a new, and even wealthier bride, 'my dear father having living and dying desired me to marry again, there being but one son by my first ever dear wife'. (This son, Carr, was rumoured to be the father of Horace Walpole, and died in 1723.) His choice was Elizabeth Felton, only daughter of Sir Thomas Felton of Playford and granddaughter and co-heir of the 3rd Earl of Suffolk.

The Hervey family fortunes were accordingly in the ascendant when John Hervey finally regained possession of the Ickworth estate in 1700. Ickworth Hall may have been in ruins, but Hervey had no shortage of alternative homes: 6 St James's Square, a newly built town house in Bury, and the Carr manor at Aswarby. John Hervey's political career was also destined to prosper.

Sir Thomas Felton, who had been Master of the Household to William and Mary, used his influence with the Duchess of Marlborough to secure a peerage for his son-in-law on the accession of Queen Anne in 1703. Hervey, who had been a Whig MP since 1694, was pleasantly surprised to be rewarded during a Tory ministry. The Duchess later recalled:

I never was concerned in making any Peer but one, and that was my *Lord Hervey*. I had made a promise to Sir Thomas Felton that if her Majesty should ever make any new Lords I would certainly use my influence that Mr Hervey should be one.... The thing was done *purely at my request* and at a time when affairs at court ran so violently against the whole party of Whigs that Mr Hervey had laid aside all hopes of the peerage.

The 1st Baron Hervey of Ickworth, who was duly elevated to the Earldom of Bristol at the coronation of George I in 1714, bore all the appearance of a rich man. Wealth on paper was, however, very different from cash in hand, and Hervey's personal account books made unhappy reading. Lady Bristol was incurably extravagant, while his large brood of children proved exceptionally expensive. Marriage portions were required for the girls, and massive

John, 1st Earl of Bristol; by J. B. van Loo, 1742 (East Corridor)

debts were incurred by the boys, all of whom were keen gamblers. Lord Bristol frequently found himself in the awkward position of borrowing from one son to pay the debts of another. In 1743 he wrote to his grandson apologising for the small size of his allowance, pointing out that after loan interest 'the whole of what will remain for me to maintain myself and this very numerous family with in all things will scarce exceed three thousand pounds per annum, a share which I hope no branch of my family can reasonably grudge me, since the world will expect that I should live something like the Earl of Bristol as your Lordship like Baron Hervey'.

It was not surprising, therefore, that the grandiose plans for a new house at Ickworth came to nothing. Lord Bristol grew to love Ickworth Lodge, the farmhouse he had converted as a temporary residence back in 1702, and became increasingly blind to its shortcomings. Money was diverted from ambitious building plans to the slow creation of a worthy park and garden, and to the adornment of existing properties. The 1st Earl was a great patron of local artists such as John Fayram and Joseph Brook, commissioning numerous paintings of his wife and family. In London he patronised better known painters such as Michael Dahl, Enoch Seeman and Sir Godfrey Kneller, and bought miniatures from Peter Cross and Bernard Lens. He also purchased a considerable amount of silver and silver-gilt, much of it in the latest richly applied and heavily ornamented style, from the leading Huguenot silversmiths David Willaume, Pierre Harache, Pierre Platel and Paul de Lamerie (now displayed in the Museum Room). More transient, but equally absorbing, was his passion for racing: Lord Bristol's most successful horse 'Wenn' won over 5,000 guineas in 21 victorious races, and was painted by Joseph Brook in 1716.

JOHN, LORD HERVEY
(1696–1743)

The 1st Earl's eldest son by his second marriage was the most successful member of an unsatisfactory brood. John, Lord Hervey, despite his early death at the age of 47, was one of the best-known figures of his time – a politician and pamphleteer of the Walpole faction, who became Vice-Chamberlain of the Royal Household and Lord Privy Seal. Lord Hervey is best remembered today for his vivid, outspoken memoirs of the court of George II, and for his devotion to Queen Caroline. He tells us that he 'made prodigious court to her, and really loved and admired her'. As for the Queen, 'she called him always her "child, her pupil, her charge"; used to tell him perpetually that his being so impertinent and daring to contradict her so continually was owing to his knowing that she could not live without him, and often said "It is well that I am so old, or I should be talked of for this creature".'

Lord Hervey's ambivalent sexuality, from his close friendship with Stephen Fox to his seduction of the Prince of Wales's mistress, attracted the attention of his contemporaries. Lady Mary Wortley Montagu came to the famous conclusion that there were three human species – 'Men, women, and Herveys'; while the poet Pope pilloried him under the name of Sporus in his *Epistle to Dr Arbuthnot*:

Let Sporus tremble – 'What? That thing of silk,
Sporus, that mere white curd of ass's milk?
Satire or sense, alas! can Sporus feel?
Who breaks a butterfly upon a wheel?'
 Yet let me flap this bug with gilded wings,
This painted child of dirt, that stinks and stings;
. . . And he himself one vile antithesis.
Amphibious thing! that acting either part,
The trifling head or the corrupted heart,
Fop at the toilet, flatterer at the board,
Now trips a lady, now struts a lord,
Eve's tempter thus the rabbins [rabbis] have express'd,
A cherub's face, a reptile all the rest,
Beauty that shocks you, parts that none can trust,
Wit that can creep, and pride that licks the dust.

The 'vile antithesis' had in fact contracted a love match in his youth with the beautiful Molly Lepel, one of Queen Caroline's maids of honour, and was the father of eight children. Although Lady Hervey's loyalty was sorely tried by her errant husband, the couple never separated, and she became universally admired for her wit and good sense. Lord Bucking-

John, Lord Hervey holding his purse of office as Lord Privy Seal; by J. B. van Loo, 1741 (Entrance Hall)

The Hervey Conversation-piece, with John, Lord Hervey (in grey coat) surrounded by his friends; by William Hogarth (Smoking Room)

ham later wrote that 'no one contributed more to the cheerful elegance of her age than Molly Lepel, Lady Hervey', while Lord Chesterfield echoed the comments of Pope, Gay and Voltaire in praising her intelligence: 'She has all the reading a woman should have and more than any woman need have; for she understands Latin perfectly well, though she wisely conceals it. No woman ever had more than she has, le ton de la parfaitement bonne compagnie, les manières engageantes et le je ne sais quoi que plaît.' Molly became a great favourite with her father-in-law, and retired to live with him at 'Sweet Ickworth' following the death of her husband in

1743. The 1st Earl attributed his son's early death to his fondness for 'that detestable and poisonous plant, tea'.

THE 2ND AND 3RD EARLS OF BRISTOL (1721–79)

The 1st Earl died at Ickworth Lodge in January 1751 at the ripe old age of 86, and was succeeded by his eldest grandson, George Hervey. The 2nd Earl followed in his father's footsteps as a prominent Whig politician, serving as Minister in Turin (1755–8), Ambassador to Madrid (1758–61), Lord Lieutenant of Ireland (1766–7) and Lord Privy Seal (1768–70). Lord Bristol's government appointments left him little time to visit the family estates, and his inordinate pride made him dismissive of the

The 2nd Earl of Bristol; by Anton Raphael Mengs, c.1761 (West Bedroom)

cramped conditions at Ickworth. An anonymous travel diary of the 1750s notes that 'his Lordship never makes any Stay here as the house is not even fit to receive a private Gentleman'. Towards the end of his life, the 2nd Earl did, however, employ Capability Brown to carry out work in the park, for which Brown received payments totalling £581 8s between 1769 and 1776. On his death in 1775, Lord Bristol was succeeded for a brief period by his next brother, Augustus, Vice-Admiral of the Blue, whose great full-length portrait by Gainsborough hangs in the Drawing Room. His racy journal covers the years between 1746 and 1759, and gives an entertaining account of his life as a naval captain, of his wartime adventures afloat, and his amorous adventures ashore. In 1744 he secretly married the notorious Elizabeth Chudleigh. Her bigamous marriage to the Duke of Kingston in 1769 caused one of the most famous scandals of the 18th century. According to Leigh Hunt, Mrs Hervey was 'an adventuress who, after playing tricks with a parish register for

the purpose of alternately falsifying and substantiating a real marriage, according as the prospects of her husband varied, imposed herself on a duke for a spinster, and survived him as his duchess till unmasked by a Court of Law.'

The 2nd and 3rd Earls may have spent little time at Ickworth, but they did add substantially to the family collections. George Hervey picked up heavily gilded furniture and portraits of Sardinian and Spanish royalty during his trips to Turin and Madrid, and amassed an impressive quantity of Ambassadorial silver in payment for his services. Augustus Hervey commissioned a series of views of his naval victories (now also in the Museum Room) from the marine artist Dominic Serres, and is thought to have received the pair of malachite-topped tables now in the Library as a gift from Catherine the Great of Russia.

THE EARL-BISHOP (1730–1803)

The 3rd Earl was succeeded in turn by his next brother, Frederick – the genial and eccentric Earl-Bishop. As a younger son, Frederick Hervey had initially tried his hand at the legal profession before transferring his ambitions to the church in 1754. Hervey's decision proved to be a fortunate one: the 2nd Earl was appointed Lord Lieutenant of Ireland in 1766, and quickly secured the Bishoprics of Cloyne (1767) and Derry (1768) for his impecunious brother. Frederick increased the income from the Derry estates to £20,000 a year by ensuring that the heavy charges for the renewal of agricultural leases were paid direct to him and not the diocese. In his early years as Bishop, Hervey displayed a notable enthusiasm for diocesan reforms and Irish Nationalism. His assistance of Roman Catholics and Presbyterians alike earned him enormous popularity with the Irish, but permanently alienated George III. The Bishop's mercurial temperament, however, did not in the end fit him to play a serious political role in Ireland. Indeed even his ecclesiastical duties seemed to many to be undertaken in an irresponsibly frivolous manner: on one famous

(Opposite page) The 3rd Earl of Bristol; by Thomas Gainsborough, 1767 (Drawing Room)

occasion he organised a curate's race along the sands at Downhill, the winners to be rewarded with vacant benefices in his diocese. His passion for travelling and collecting works of art also led to more and more prolonged absences from Ireland, and he soon became a well-known figure bowling along the roads of Germany and Italy in his great coach, causing the name of Bristol to be given to hotels in towns all over Europe.

Hervey puzzled and amazed his contemporaries. Sir Jonah Barrington described him as 'a man of elegant erudition, extensive learning, and an enlightened and classical, but eccentric mind: – bold, ardent, and versatile; he dazzled the vulgar by ostentatious state, and worked apon [sic] the gentry by ease and condescension'. The Irish peer Lord Charlemont was more damming: 'His genius is like a shallow stream, rapid, noisy, diverting, but useless. Such is his head, and I fear it is much superior to his heart. He is proud and to the last degree vindictive; vain to excess, inconstant in his friendships . . . his ambition and his lust can alone get the better of his avarice.'

Few of these characteristics made the Earl-Bishop an easy husband or father. Hervey's long-suffering wife Elizabeth was the daughter of Sir Jermyn Davers, heir to the ancient Jermyn seat of Rushbrook Hall in Suffolk. Their marriage had been opposed by both sets of parents – the Daverses because Hervey was a younger son, and the Herveys because Sir Jermyn had married his wife only after the birth of several illegitimate children. Elizabeth

The Earl-Bishop before a vista of Rome; by Hugh Douglas Hamilton, 1790 (West Bedroom)

Hervey followed her husband from Suffolk to Ireland, and on endless continental tours, before finally agreeing to separate in 1782, after quarrelling during a carriage-ride from Ickworth. They never spoke again. The Bishop enjoyed good relationships with his two elder daughters – Lady Erne and Lady Elizabeth Foster – but quarrelled with both his sons. The elder, John Augustus, died in 1796 after a scandalous spell as Ambassador to Florence, while he never forgave the younger, Frederick William, for refusing to marry the illegitimate daughter of the King of Prussia.

Ultimately, family came second to Hervey's twin passions – building and collecting. His income as Bishop of Derry had already allowed him to build a vast mansion at Downhill on the north coast of Co. Londonderry in 1775, and to fill his diocese with new churches, spires and bridges. The inheritance of the Bristol titles and estates in 1779 encouraged the Earl-Bishop (as he was subsequently known) to new excesses: indulging his fascination for oval buildings, huge rotundas with flanking wings were begun at Ballyscullion in Co. Londonderry in 1787 and at Ickworth in 1795. Galleries at these two houses were intended to display the fruits of a lifetime of obsessive collecting. In 1796 Lord Bristol summed up his intentions as follows:

The idea I have struck out, of showing the historical progress of the art of painting in all the five different schools of Germany & Italy, I deem both happy & instructive. Galleries in general are both confused & uninstructive. Mine, by placing the authors under different schools, will show the characteristick excellence of each, instruct the young mind & edify the old.

Sadly, the Earl-Bishop's magnificent collection was destined to remain in Italy. Confiscated by Napoleonic troops in Rome in 1798, it was dispersed by auction in 1804. Lord Bristol spent the last years of his life campaigning for its restitution, dying on the road to Albano in 1803, in the outhouse of an Italian farmer who refused to admit a Protestant bishop into his house. By a final stroke of irony that would probably have delighted him, when his coffin came to be shipped back to the family vault at Ickworth, it had to be disguised as the packing case for an antique statue, the superstitious sailors refusing to have a corpse on board.

The 1st Marquess of Bristol; by John Hoppner (Dining Room)

THE 1ST MARQUESS (1769–1859)

The Earl-Bishop's youngest son, Frederick William, was a very different man from his father, of whom he had seen little during his childhood. Frederick was only thirteen when his parents separated in 1782, and he and his sister Louisa had been brought up by their mother, then living in virtual seclusion at Ickworth. Life was transformed for this sober and restrained young man in 1796, when his flamboyant elder brother, Lord Hervey, died suddenly at sea.

The new Viscount Hervey found himself almost immediately in conflict with his father, who became determined to marry him off to the immensely wealthy illegitimate daughter of the King of Prussia. To the chagrin of his volatile parent, Hervey refused to break off his existing engagement to the Hon. Elizabeth Upton, and the couple were married in 1798. This sense of commitment to responsibilities was to characterise Frederick's career; he immediately took on the Herveys' political role in Bury, sitting as MP from 1796 to 1803, and served the Addington government as an Under-Secretary of State for the Foreign Office, where his brother-in-law, the future Prime Minister, Lord Liverpool, was Foreign Secretary.

The Earl-Bishop's death in 1803 brought new burdens. The 5th Earl found himself heir only to the entailed English estates, while the Earl-Bishop's huge personal fortune and his property in Ireland was left to a distant cousin, Henry Hervey-Bruce. All that the new Lord Bristol received, under the designation 'my ungrateful and undutyful son', was a derisory £1,000. Building work on the Rotunda at Ickworth came to an immediate halt while he gloomily took stock of his position. Lord Liverpool was confident that his brother-in-law would win through. In August 1803 he wrote to George III asserting that the Bristol estates were 'capable of considerable improvement, and though there are some heavy burdens upon them, they are of such a nature as by the prudence and good sense of the present proprietor will soon be removed'.

Lord Liverpool's confidence was not misplaced. By 1819 Lord Bristol's finances had recovered sufficiently to allow the complete rebuilding of the London house in St James's Square, and in 1821 construction work on the Rotunda was finally continued. Both projects were designed and supervised by John Field, a London builder turned architect who maintained an obsequious correspondence with his patron. In 1829 the recently created 1st Marquess also set about rebuilding his house at Brighton, which duly became the third of his properties to be completely furnished and decorated by the royal furniture makers Banting, France & Co. Although Bantings worked extensively for the Prince Regent and William IV, Ickworth contains the most comprehensive range of their products now known. Lord Bristol admired their distinctive heavily carved mahogany and rosewood furniture, and continued to commission new pieces until his death in 1859. The firm also acted as restorers and inventory-takers for his son and grandson, undertaking their final work at Ickworth in 1899.

If the 1st Marquess was to complete his father's grandiose plans for Ickworth, suitable works of art had to be found to replace the Earl-Bishop's lost

collections. Lord Bristol accordingly took his wife and young family on an extended tour of Europe, from July 1817 to May 1821. The family travelled through France, Belgium, Germany, Switzerland and Italy, before settling in Paris for a year in 1820. Lord Bristol commissioned busts from Bartolini in Florence, drawings from Rehberg in Rome, and purchased porcelain, clocks and furniture in Paris. He was also able to buy back one of the Earl-Bishop's best known sculptures – Flaxman's *Fury of Athamas* – and may have acquired the impressive group of Spanish paintings now at Ickworth, including examples by Velázquez and Ribera.

THE 3RD MARQUESS (1834–1907)

The 2nd Marquess of Bristol outlived his father by only five years, and was succeeded in 1864 by his dependable eldest son, Frederick William, Earl Jermyn. The 3rd Marquess enjoyed a brief Com-

Geraldine, Marchioness of Bristol holding one of her collection of fans, which are displayed on the Museum Landing; by Henry Graves, 1870 (Museum Landing)

The family taking breakfast in the Library in the mid-19th century

mons career as MP for West Suffolk (1859–64) before devoting his attention to county and estate affairs. He was Lord Lieutenant of Suffolk for over twenty years, and a keen supporter of the Suffolk Sheep Society. His wife, Geraldine Anson, was well known in her day for her collection of antique fans, one of the largest to remain in a country house (now displayed on the Museum Landing).

Although the 3rd Marquess suffered financial setbacks in his later years, he was initially able to keep Ickworth in good repair, and even to undertake some improvements. Soon after inheriting, he approached the architect F.C. Penrose for a full report on the condition of the house. The resulting lengthy schedule of repairs and alterations marked the start of a 25-year involvement, beginning with consolidation work to the roof of the dome. Plans for a magnificent new staircase in the Rotunda were

eventually abandoned, but Penrose was able to persuade Lord Bristol to complete the interior of the unfinished West Corridor, creating a striking 'New Room' known today as the Pompeian Room.

The scheme appears to have been conceived as a tribute to Lord Bristol's great-grandfather, the Earl-Bishop. One of the 4th Earl's more unusual purchases had been a series of original Roman frescoes, excavated at the Villa Negroni in Rome in the 1770s. The frescoes themselves, destined for Downhill, appear to have been lost, but a set of hand-coloured engravings dedicated to the Earl-Bishop was preserved at Ickworth. The fashionable decorative artist John Dibblee Crace was employed to decorate the walls of the room with idealised versions of these wall-paintings, while the West Corridor and Ante-Room were picked out with subtle stencilled and lined decoration in toning colours.

The 4th Marquess of Bristol; by Sir Arthur Cope (Dining Room)

THE 4TH MARQUESS (1863–1951) AND MARCHIONESS (1875–1957)

The 3rd Marquess had two daughters, but no son, and so the Ickworth estate and the Bristol title passed to a nephew, Frederick Hervey. Frederick's parents, Lord and Lady Augustus Hervey, had been key members of the 'Marlborough House Set' which gathered round the Prince of Wales in the 1870s. The new Lord Bristol showed little inclination for high society and pursued a successful naval career, retiring with the rank of Rear-Admiral. His wife, Theodora, was the granddaughter of the Victorian railway contractor George Wythes, and devoted most of her immense personal fortune to the improvement of Ickworth.

The 4th Marquess and Marchioness carried out considerable alterations to Ickworth between 1909 and 1911. Lady Bristol was appalled by the cramped conditions of the servants' quarters in the East Wing, the lack of electricity or proper bathrooms, and the unfinished state of many bedrooms in the Rotunda. The architect A. C. Blomfield was called in to remedy these deficiencies, and to suggest ways of updating the 1st Marquess's great state rooms. Blomfield's solution was to demolish John Field's central stone staircase, and to open up the rear wall of the Entrance Hall, allowing more light into the centre of the building. Regency paint schemes of stone and pink were replaced with bright Edwardian whites, blues and pale greens, and textiles rewoven in brilliant jewel colours. The colours were chosen by the Marchioness, as her husband was colour-blind.

Lady Bristol was equally concerned by the condition of the contents of the house. The picture collection was catalogued, cleaned and rehung, under the aegis of a local expert, Edward Farrer. The book collection was listed and re-bound by Birdsall's of London, and the furniture and *objets d'art* thoroughly restored. Lady Bristol also compiled scrapbooks of pictures and sculpture associated with the Hervey family, and sought to purchase any of these which came on the market. Notable successes include the large group of Jermyn and Davers portraits from Rushbrook Hall, and the Earl-Bishop's commissions for Downhill bought at the sale of Margaret, Lady Bruce in 1950.

THE NATIONAL TRUST (FROM 1956)

In 1956, five years after the death of the 4th Marquess, the house and 1,792 acres of the estate (including the park and many acres of woodland), together with the greater part of the splendid collection of furniture, pictures and other works of art, were accepted by the Treasury in lieu of death duties and handed over to the National Trust. The Marchioness of Bristol gave a generous endowment to the Trust for the maintenance of the house and property. Her daughters, Lady Marjorie Erskine and Lady Phyllis Macrae, continued to farm the estate until the 1970s.

THE BUILDING OF ICKWORTH

ICKWORTH HALL (–1702)

Until the Civil War, the owners of the Ickworth estate lived in a substantial fortified manor house immediately to the east of Ickworth church. Although the house was demolished about 1702, the outline of the foundations remained visible for many years as a parch mark during dry summers. Lord Arthur Hervey, a keen member of the Bury and West Suffolk Archaeological Institute, plotted the marks in 1844, and his findings were confirmed by excavation in 1986.

The site appears to have been occupied since at least the 13th century, when a small half-timbered hall formed the home of the de Ickworth family. From the 16th century onwards, a series of brick additions and alterations were made by the Herveys. A tower porch was attached to the entrance façade, ornamented with moulded bricks. Wings were added to the original hall, creating an imposing U-shaped house, comparable in size and plan to Kentwell Hall, near Long Melford in Suffolk. In front of the house was a base-court, protected by a surrounding wall and approached through a gateway.

Kentwell Hall, which the original Ickworth Hall closely resembled

Ickworth Hall remained the family seat until 1642, when Sir William Hervey married the wealthy widow Lady Penelope Gage, and retired to her home, Hengrave Hall. The hall appears to have been let to a succession of tenants and remained in good condition until at least 1665, when an estate survey recorded that the 'Chief Mansion house called Ickworth Hall with a large Barne, a Stable, a Dovehouse … a large orchard and gardines' was tenanted by one Edward Baythorne.

Neglect seems to have finally set in in the 1680s with the inheritance of John Hervey's wife, the Hon. Elizabeth Hervey of Kidbrooke, who had retired abroad and showed little concern for her estate. By the time of her death in 1700 it was found that Mrs Hervey's agents, among other great 'wastes', had 'suffered the seat of the family to run into such ruine and decay that daily the tiles, sometimes by loads, fall off the Mansion-house, whereby the timber-roofs have lain so expos'd to the sun and rain, that they being rotten fall down, and have destroyed the planchard floors, which now in some places lie upon one another'.

ICKWORTH LODGE AND PLANS FOR A NEW HOUSE (1702–95)

From 1702 to 1828 the Hervey family lived, with varying degrees of discomfort, in a converted farmhouse known as Ickworth Lodge. Finding the old hall uninhabitable, the 1st Earl (1665–1751) hurriedly extended a house on Ickworth Green; an oil painting of c.1780 records an E-shaped building, composed of an eight-bay central block, flanked by projecting wings, and decorated with battlements. Although large enough to accommodate Hervey's immediate household of 49, visitors and family alike thought little of the lodge. The architect Sir Thomas Robinson, who visited in 1731, described the house as 'a tenant's old house in the park, so very bad a habitation, that I am astonished how so large a family have so long made a shift in it'.

The 1st Earl was keen to build a new house worthy of the Hervey name. Initially, he consulted William Talman, then engaged with work for the Duke of Newcastle at Houghton in Norfolk and Welbeck in Nottinghamshire. Talman was quickly supplanted by his arch-rival Sir John Vanbrugh, even though plans had reached an advanced stage. Vanbrugh reported to the Duke of Newcastle in June 1703 that 'My Lord Hervey has gone much further than your Grace has done, tho' he has not actually laid his foundations yet'.

Vanbrugh's first task appears to have been to prevent his client from choosing a new, and in his view inferior, site. Lord Hervey toyed with the idea of buying the Jermyn seat, Rushbrook, but quickly reverted to his original scheme, writing to Vanbrugh in July 1703:

I desire you may have the case of knowing that Risbrook rather declines than improves in its unequal competition with Ickworth; for I find ye latter such a sort of beauty as – si proprius stes, te capiet magis [the closer you get to it, the more it appeals], and from thence feel so strong propensions to make it so much a more noble seat than the other is capable of that less persuasive reasons would have secured my choice than were by you employed.

Two months later Lord Hervey ordered 120 tons of Ketton stone from Rutland, and all appeared set for building work to start.

Quite why the plans went no further remains a mystery. Sir Thomas Robinson, writing in 1731, reported that 'the old mansion was pulled down about twenty years ago, and those materials and others sufficient to build a new house were led to another situation, and the new one determined to be built; but an ill run at play (as fame reports) stopped the design, and most of the wood, brick and stone have since been used in tenants houses'. A letter among the Elveden papers, dated March 1796, is more specific:

Ickworth Park House – this was intended to have been built many years ago by John 1st Earl and the stones were accordingly brought from Ketton as I have been told all by Land Carriage. . . . One night her Ladyship coming home a little flustered, my lord asked her the reason. Found she had lost £30000 at Play. There is no more to be said the Coach must come tomorrow and carry us to the Country and the new house must be given up.

Ickworth Lodge, from a painting of c.1780

The Earl-Bishop's Ballyscullion in Co. Londonderry, which provided the model for Ickworth

Although there is no direct evidence for massive losses in 1703, Hervey's diary for that year records a resolve to give up gambling for ever, listing seven reasons for it being a 'Bad Thing'.

The future Earl of Bristol may have been able to control his own expenditure, but he never succeeded in curbing the extravagance of his wife, or his numerous and unsatisfactory sons. A further set of plans was commissioned from Vanbrugh in 1718, but after that nothing more was heard of the new house, and Lord Bristol's ever-delayed intention of building became a society joke. He did, however, proceed with the construction of large walled gardens and a formal canal near the site of the old hall. The small summer-house which forms the centrepiece of this layout, and where Lord Bristol loved to practise his flute, is very much in the style of Talman, and may date back to the original plans of *c.*1702.

THE ROTUNDA (1795–1803)

In 1779 the 1st Earl's third grandson, Frederick Augustus, Bishop of Derry, succeeded his brother as 4th Earl of Bristol. Here, finally, was the man to complete the Bristol seat, albeit in a manner very different from that intended by his grandfather. The new Lord Bristol had spent many years touring the Continent, purchasing paintings and sculpture on the widest scale; Ickworth, like the vast Irish houses he built at Downhill and Ballyscullion, was conceived rather as a museum to contain these works of art, than for domestic comfort.

The Earl-Bishop lived at Ickworth for only two short periods following his inheritance, but on both occasions considered grandiose schemes for rebuilding. During his first extended stay in 1781–2 he consulted Capability Brown and commissioned 'Plans and elevations for an Intire New House'. These plans, now lost, appear to have come to nothing after the Earl-Bishop quarrelled bitterly with his wife. His second visit, in 1792, was more successful. Inspired with new desire to build a house on the site originally suggested by Brown, the Earl-Bishop returned to Italy in search of an appropriate architect. His instructions were specific: to repeat, and improve, the extraordinary plans that he had developed at Ballyscullion for a domed oval rotunda with curved corridors leading to rectangular wings. This strange design, by the Irish architect Michael Shanahan, was loosely based on Belle Isle – a circular house built by John Plaw in 1775 on an island in Lake Windermere. The curved corridors, with attached wings, were added at Lord Bristol's suggestion, and were drawn from Bernini's colonnades at St Peter's in Rome.

The Earl-Bishop is thought to have approached several architects in Rome, including the young Charles Heathcote Tatham, before finally fixing on

The model of Ickworth was probably made to send to the Earl-Bishop in Italy for his approval

Mario Asprucci the Younger (1764–1804). Two of Asprucci's original drawings for Ickworth have survived, dated to late 1794 and early 1795. Both relate closely to Ballyscullion, but indicate a building much larger in scale, with more lavish use of ornament. Asprucci envisaged bas-relief sculpture at two levels on the Rotunda, and running along the corridors, with sculpture in niches below.

Asprucci's designs, drawn up in Italy, were adapted and simplified in England by Francis Sandys. Sandys and his brother Joseph had already worked for Lord Bristol at Ballyscullion, and were familiar with their patron's unusual demands. Although building work began in late 1795, the final design was not agreed until 1796, when the brothers (known affectionately as 'my young hounds') prepared a model for the Earl-Bishop's approval. Sculptural ornament was confined to the Rotunda only, while the portico was reduced in size and given a pediment. Most importantly, the curv-

ing corridors were made to join the Rotunda farther north, rather than in the centre – a concession to the English climate, allowing more southern light into the main ground-floor rooms.

Lord Bristol's own involvement in the architectural details of his new house can be gauged by his voluminous correspondence on the subject. The alteration to the position of the corridors was one of the few non-Italianate features allowed. The Earl-Bishop was determined that traditional Palladian stucco should be used on the exterior, and chose Italian craftsmen to execute the terracotta reliefs for the two friezes on the Rotunda. He was equally insistent on the massive scale of the new house, and specified the internal and external dimensions. In 1796 he wrote to his friend John Symonds:

I have fixed on 30 feet for the height of my parlour floor from observing that my Lungs always played more freely, my spirits spontaneously rose much higher in lofty rooms than in low ones, where the atmosphere is too much tainted with the atmosphere of our own bodies, & also for the sake of throwing my attick-story (if possible) into St Paul's 3rd Heaven.

What were the Earl-Bishop's motives in building a palace on so large a scale, with such magnificent adornment? Familial pride and dynastic ambition certainly provide part of the answer. A far more compelling reason for both the size of the house, and its curious plan, however, was the Earl-Bishop's mania for collecting. Ickworth was to be a potent combination of family seat and museum. Living accommodation was to be provided in the Rotunda, while the wings were to be devoted to didactic galleries. Writing to John Symonds in July 1796 he concluded:

I wish to unite magnificence with convenience and simplicity with dignity – no redundancy – no super-fluity – no one unnecessary room, but the necessary ones to be noble and convenient, to have few pictures but choice ones, and my galleries to exhibit an histori-cal progress of the art of Painting both in Germany and Italy, and that divided into its characteristical schools – Venice, Bologna, Florence etc.

In the next two years he feverishly collected works of art for Ickworth. By early 1798 he had assembled (in his own estimation) an 'immense and valuable and beautiful property of large mosaic pavements, sumptuous chimney pieces for my new house, and pictures, statues, busts and marbles with-out end, first rate Titians and Raphaels, dear Guidoes, and three old Caraccis – Gran Dio, che tesoro'. Sadly, none of these treasures was ever to reach Ickworth. In 1798 the French invaded Italy; the Earl-Bishop's collections were confiscated, and he himself imprisoned in Milan for nine months. A petition was signed by 323 artists living in Rome calling for the release of the collections, but it was to no avail. The majority of them was later auctioned in Rome.

It is a testament to the strength of the Earl-Bishop's vision for Ickworth that he did not abandon construction at this point. Instead, work continued apace, while he remained on the Continent, pur-chasing what he could, and campaigning for the restitution of his goods. Even so, all that was finished by the time of the Earl-Bishop's sudden death in 1803 was the shell of the Rotunda, standing alone on bare ground, as if uprooted from Italy.

ICKWORTH HOUSE COMPLETED (1821–41)

After the Earl-Bishop's death, his son Frederick William Hervey had to stop work on the new house for lack of money. For the next twenty years the unfinished Rotunda was a tourist attraction much noted by contemporary diarists and travel guides. The author of *The Beauties of England* reported in 1813 that 'The interior of this neglected edifice exhibits a mere shell, with a kind of open staircase to ascend the roof and take a view of the adjacent country', while 'the wings, and the galleries connecting them with the edifice in the centre, have been run up to the height of only three or four feet'.

It was not until the 1820s that improvements in estate income allowed the 1st Marquess to consider completing his father's ambitious plans. Although most travel guides assumed that his first wish was to demolish the unwieldy structure, and sell the mate-rials for scrap, his personal letters reveal a lengthy struggle to assemble enough funds to begin the project. In 1819 he wrote to his eldest son 'what you say of the new house at Ickworth makes me regret

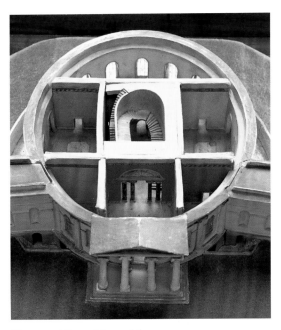

The ground floor of the model

that I had not money enough to complete the body next year. ... If I could have mustered five or six thousand pounds I would have begun it directly, but I must have patience.'

Although the 1st Marquess chose to adhere to the overall spirit of the designs worked up by Asprucci and Sandys for the Earl-Bishop, his reasons for building were very different. Having endured nearly twenty years in the cramped quarters of Ickworth Lodge, he was concerned primarily to create a comfortable and convenient family home. The 105-foot-high Rotunda, with its provision for 30-foot-high rooms, was highly unsuitable for this purpose. He accordingly asked his architect, the London builder John Field, to reverse the Earl-Bishop's plan. The wings were no longer required for gallery space, and the family accommodation, with small, ornately decorated rooms, could be fitted into the East Wing. The West Wing was completed purely for the sake of symmetry, with an Orangery inserted on the south front.

Lord Bristol did not, however, entirely abandon his father's dream of Ickworth as a 'temple of the arts'. John Field was also instructed to complete the

The unfinished interior of the dome

ground floor of the Rotunda, creating tall austere rooms ideal for the display of the larger family portraits and dramatic history paintings. The cavernous Entrance Hall, with its giant scagliola columns, was deliberately designed as a framework for Flaxman's colossal marble group, *The Fury of Athamas*.

Although building work began in 1821, the project was unusually protracted due to a series of financial crises. Lord Bristol was never certain of obtaining enough estate income to pay the next bill, and some payments had to be financed by panic sales of land. In 1826, the year he was created a Marquess, he wrote to his son 'God help you my dearest Hervey – your mother is much better – so am I, but I shall be better when these sales are over and the essential part of the new house up and paid for – I have lived so long upon this stretch that I feel sometimes as if I should fail suddenly'. The 1st Marquess and his family finally moved into the East Wing in 1829, but work in the Rotunda continued until 1832, and the West Wing was completed only in 1841.

(Left) The Rotunda in 1818 as inherited by the 1st Marquess, with the wings not yet built

BIBLIOGRAPHY

The Hervey family papers are on deposit at the Suffolk Record Office, Bury St Edmunds.

ANON., 'French Furniture at Ickworth', *Apollo*, December 1956, pp. 203–7.

BANISTER, Judith, 'Rococo Silver in a Neo-Classical Setting: The Bristol Family Silver at Ickworth', *Country Life*, 4 September 1980, pp. 792–4.

CHILDE-PEMBERTON, W. S., *The Earl Bishop*, London, 1924.

CORNFORTH, John, 'Ickworth, Suffolk', *Country Life*, 19, 26 August 1999, pp. 40–5, 42–5.

ERSKINE, David, ed., *Augustus Hervey's Journal, 1746–59*, London, 1953.

FARRER, Edmund, *Portraits in Suffolk Houses (West)*, London, 1908, pp. 199–230.

FIGGIS, Nicola, 'The Roman Property of Frederick Augustus Hervey, 4th Earl of Bristol and Bishop of Derry (1730–1803)', *Walpole Society*, lv, 1992–3.

FORD, Brinsley, 'The Earl Bishop, an Eccentric and Capricious Patron of the Arts', *Apollo*, xcix, June 1974, pp. 426–34.

FOTHERGILL, Brian, *The Mitred Earl: An Eighteenth-Century Eccentric*, London, 1974.

GAGE, John, *History and Antiquities of Suffolk (Thingoe Hundred)*, 1838, pp. 272–322.

GORE, St John, 'Pictures at Ickworth', *Country Life*, 3, 10 December 1964, pp. 1508–12, 1654–6.

HALSBAND, Robert, *Lord Hervey: Eighteenth-Century Courtier*, Oxford, 1973.

HERVEY, Lord Arthur, 'The Family of Hervey', *Proceedings of Suffolk Institute of Archaeology*, ii, 1859, pp. 293–434.

HERVEY, S. H. A., ed., *The Diary of John Hervey*, Bury St Edmunds, 1894.

HERVEY, S. H. A., ed., *Letter Books of John Hervey, 1st Earl of Bristol, 1681–1750*, Bury St Edmunds, 1894.

HERVEY, S. H. A., ed., 'Diary of the Hon. William Hervey', *Suffolk Green Books*, xiv, 1906.

HOLMES, Michael, *Augustus Hervey: A Naval Casanova*, Bishop Auckland, 1996.

HOWARD, Seymour, 'Boy on a Dolphin: Nollekens and Cavaceppi', *Art Bulletin*, June 1964, pp. 177–89.

HUSSEY, Christopher, 'Ickworth, Suffolk', *Country Life*, 10 March 1955, pp. 678–81.

ILCHESTER, Earl of, ed., *Lord Hervey and his Friends*, London, 1950.

JOY, E. T., 'Furniture in the East Wing at Ickworth', *Connoisseur*, June 1971, pp. 77–85.

KENWORTHY-BROWNE, John, 'Sculptor and Revolutionary: British Portraits by Bartolini', *Country Life*, 8 June 1978, pp. 1655–6.

LINES, R. Charles, 'Ickworth', *Connoisseur*, March 1958, pp. 69–73.

PENZER, N. M., 'The Hervey Silver at Ickworth', *Apollo*, February, March 1957, pp. 39–43, 133–7.

PONSONBY, D. A., *Call a Dog Hervey*, London, 1949.

RANKIN, Peter, *Irish Building Ventures of the Earl Bishop of Derry*, Ulster Architectural Heritage Society, 1972.

SHOBERL, Frederick, *A Topographical and Historical Description of the County of Suffolk*, London, 1820.

STRACHEY, Nino, 'The Pompeian Room at Ickworth: The Work of F. C. Penrose and J. D. Crace', *Apollo*, May 1997, pp. 8–12.

TIGHE, W. J., 'The Herveys: Three Generations of Tudor Courtiers', *Proceedings of the Suffolk Institute of Archaeology and History*, xxxvi, part 1, 1985.

TIPPING, H. A., 'Ickworth, Suffolk', *Country Life*, 31 October, 7 November 1925, pp. 668–75, 698–705.

TUDOR-CRAIG, Pamela, 'The Evolution of Ickworth', *Country Life*, 17 May 1973, pp. 1362–5.

WILLOUGHBY, Leonard, 'The Marquess of Bristol's Collection at Ickworth', *Connoisseur*, April, May, June 1906, pp. 203–10, 3–10, 84–90.

HERVEY FAMILY TREE

JOHN HERVEY OF ICKWORTH (1490–1556) = Elizabeth Pope of Mildenha Suffolk

WILLIAM (1526–92) = Elizabeth Poley Boxted (d. 1616)

JOHN (1562–1630) = Frances Bocking of Ashbocking, Suffol (d. 1620)

Sir WILLIAM* (1585/6–1660) = (1) Susan Jermyn* (d. 1637), dau. of Sir Robert Jermyn of Rushbrook Hall, Suffolk m. 1612 = (2) Lady Penelope Rivers* (d. 1661), heiress of Thomas, Earl Rivers, of Hengrave Hall, Suffolk m. 1642 = (1) Sir George Trenchard (d. 161 (2) Sir George Gage, 1st Bt (d. 1633)

JOHN* (1616–79) = ELIZABETH HERVEY* (c.1615–1700)   William* (1619–42)   Sir Thomas* (1625–94) = Isabella May* (1625–86), dau. of Sir Humphrey Ma Vice-Chamberlain in the household of Charles I

Thomas (1668–95)   3 daus.

JOHN* (1665–1751) cr. BARON HERVEY 1703 and 1st EARL OF BRISTOL 1714 = (1) Isabella Carr* (1670–93), dau. and heiress of Sir Robert Carr, Bt, of Sleaford, Lincs. m. 1688 = (2) Elizabeth Felton* (1676–1741) m. 169

Carr, Lord Hervey* (1691–1723)   Isabella Carr* (1689–1711)   Elizabeth (1693–5)   John, Lord Hervey* (1696–1743) = Mary Lepel* (1696–1768), dau. of Brig.-General Nicholas Lepel m. 1720   Elizabeth* (1697–1727) = Hon. Bus Mansel

GEORGE WILLIAM 2nd EARL OF BRISTOL* (1721–75)   Lepel* (1723–80) = Constantine Phipps, Lord Mulgrave* (1722–75)   Kitty ~ Hunter*   AUGUSTUS JOHN 3rd EARL OF BRISTOL* (1724–79) = Elizabeth Chudleigh* (1720–88) m. 1744 m. bigamously Duke of Kingston 1769   Mary* (1726–1815) m. 1745 = George Fitzgeral of Turlough Park Co. Mayo (d. 178

Augustus* (c.1765–82)

Mary* (1753–1842) m. 1776 = John 1st Earl Erne (1731–1828)   John Augustus Lord Hervey* (1757–96) = Elizabeth Drummond* (d. 1818) m. 1779   Elizabeth Christiana* (1759–1824) = (1) John Thomas Foster, MP m. 1776 = (2) William Cavendish 5th Duke of Devonsh (1743–1811) m. 1809

Elizabeth Caroline May* (1779–1856) = James Stuart Wortley, cr. 1st Baron Wharncliffe (1776–1845) m. 1799   Elizabeth Catherine Caroline* (1780–1803) = Charles Rose Ellis, Lord Seaford* (1771–1845)   Augusta* (1798–1880) = Frederick Seymour (1797–1856)   FREDERICK WILLIAM (EARL JERMYN) 2nd MARQUESS OF BRISTOL* (1800–64) = Lady Katherine Isabella Manners* (1809–48), dau. of 5th Duke of Rutla m. 1830

Charles Augustus, 6th Lord Howard de Walden (1799–1868)   Eliza* (d. 1896)   FREDERICK WILLIAM JOHN* 3rd MARQUESS OF BRISTOL (1834–1907) = Geraldine Anson* (1843–192 dau. of General the Hon. George Anson m. 1862

Katherine (d. 1948) = Alan Drummond (d. 1913)   Alice (d. 1962) = 3rd Baron Hylton (d. 1945)   Charles Henry Augustus* (1862–93)   FREDERICK WILLIAM 4th MARQUESS OF BRISTOL* (1863–1951) = Alice Frances Theodora Wythe (1875–1957), dau. of George Wythes of Copped Hall m. 189

Marjorie* (1898–1967) = Lord Erskine (1895–1953)   Phyllis* (1899–1989) = Capt. Duncan MacRae (d. 1966)

Owners of Ickworth are in CAPITALS   Asterisk denotes a portrait in the house

ICKWORTH

There are 1,800 acres of park, wood and farmland at Ickworth. Horringer Park, the Deer Park and most of the roads and tracks are available for walking and recreation by the public. There are additional waymarked walks which correspond to the coloured and dotted lines on the map overleaf. You are advised to wear stout footwear for winter walks in the woods.

Please keep dogs on leads in the Park and please refrain from picking wild flowers. The Park is open every day from 7.00am until 7.00pm.

Fredrick 4th Earl of Bristol

History.

For most of the Middle Ages Ickworth was a possession of St. Edmundsbury abbey. The estate came into the hands of the Hervey family in the 15th century and has been their home ever since, although ownership of the house, park and estate passed to the National Trust on the death of the 4th Marquess of Bristol in 1956 (the Earldom of Bristol was granted to John Hervey in 1714 and the 5th Earl was created 1st Marquess in 1826). There is evidence of a deer park at Ickworth as early as 1259 - 64 and beneath much of the present parkland earthworks indicate ancient field systems and roadways. The original site of Ickworth village is uncertain but the old manor house stood close to the church on the east side. The house was demolished by the 1st Earl in 1710; the intention seems to have been to build a replacement nearby, the family decamping to Ickworth Lodge, the house of a former tenant for the duration of the works. The architects William Talman and Sir John Vanbrugh were consulted in turn but the Earl's plans for the house were never realised. In the event it was not until 1796 that the 4th Earl of Bristol, Bishop of Derry, eccentric, inveterate traveller and impassioned art collector began to build the present house, on an entirely different site.

The changing landscape.

Between 1769 and 1776 the 2nd Earl made a number of payments to the landscape gardener 'Capability' Brown. Frustratingly there are no records of the work that he undertook at Ickworth, but it seems likely that he made improvements both to the gardens around Ickworth Lodge, the family's temporary residence, and to the general layout of the park. The alterations to the park predate the building of the rotunda, and it is not clear whether or not at that time the site of the

ICKWORTH PARK WALKS
THE NATIONAL TRUST

JH 1989/91

KEY
PARK BANK, PIT etc.
hedge
PARK hedge
SCALE in miles ½ ½

WALKS:
RED Walk, the Grand Tour — eight miles; (TIMINGS e.g. 2hrs.5m, TAKEN CLOCKWISE FROM THE CAR PARK, are DELIBERATELY SLOW.)
BLUE Walk: COMPLETE CIRCUIT four miles;
ORANGE-Albana-Walk: two miles;
.... headland drove (not N.T.)
.... OTHER PATHS.
ROADS etc.;
= sealed surface, suitable for wheelchairs & buggies;
=== un- sealed track.
VIEWPOINTS.
X GATE or STILE.

d remnants of the First Mar- quess's dam;
M—above—Mordaboy's Cottage;
S the Summerhouse, c.1703,
ICKWORTH CHURCH (private)

ENTRANCE TO PARK

BURY ST ED-MUNDS
GREEN—A143
VILLAGE
HORRINGER CHURCH
ICKWORTH CHURCH
HORRINGER PARK
ELIZABETH GROVE
TURNER'S GORSE
GATE LODGE
TUCKET KIOSK
CAR AND PLAY-GROUND
Tea Party Oak
cricket pitch
oaks
Geraldine's Walk
ABDIKIN'S WOOD
ash oak
A143 HAVERHILL
LADY KATHERINE'S WOOD
Conifers
THE FAIRY LAKE
LADY HERVEY'S WOOD
gravel drive
KINDERLEE GROVE
beeches
Mansion Meadow
BUILDING PLANTATION
ICKWORTH HOUSE
JERMYN'S CLUMP
CANAL WALK
Round House
LOWNDE WOOD
RANDAN WOOD
Toy Cottage
Martin's Green
pasture with oaks—PRIVATE land—
tall oaks
beech wood
CHEVING-TON FIELD PLANTATION
steep ditch—
Chevington Lodge
STONEY HILL PLANTATION
DOWNTER'S WOOD
flint drive
White House
DAIRY WOOD
HORSEPOOL WOOD
TWIST WOOD
Horsepool Farm PLANTATION
PRESERVATION
The Valley
firm sandy track
Park River LINNET
ROUND HILL
ALBANA WOOD
ancient oak
The Bothy
conifers
ICKWORTH LODGE
ICE HOUSE HILL
pines
Saxham End
Dairy Wood Cottage
COACH ROAD PLANTATION
COACHROAD Lodge
MORDABOY'S BELT
MORDABOY'S WOOD
NEW WARREN WOOD
Bear's Meadow
PESTLE WOOD
ARTHUR'S WOOD
drive

Centre of the new Mansion erecting by Earl of Bristol at Ickworth Park near Bury Suffolk 18 Oct 1828.

Ickworth Lodge.

A large farmhouse which was the Bristol family home from 1710 until 1828 when it was converted into a rectory by Lord Arthur Hervey. Now a private retirement home.

The Obelisk.

On the southern boundary of the park. About 50 ft tall, and built to the memory of the Earl - Bishop by the people of Londonderry in 1817. See map for translation of inscription.

The Tea Party Oak.

A huge and ancient pollard under which the Horringer School treats were held for half a century from 1860.

Facilities.

The Restaurant and shop are located in the Rotunda and are open when the House is open, as are the lavatories. There are lavatories in the park, near the Walled Garden (not open during the Winter). A children's play area is located near the main car park and there is a hide overlooking the deer enclosure.

corridors and wings to conform generally with the original design after 1824. The wings were intended to house the Earl Bishop's great collection of art treasures which he had assembled in Europe; sadly the collection, worth an estimated £20,000 at the time, was confiscated by the French army in 1798 during its occupation of Rome. Now one wing is the home of the present Marquess while the other remains an empty shell. The National Trust hopes to create a new restaurant, shop and visitor reception area within the wing. The Rotunda is richly furnished and contains magnificent collections of pictures and silver. It is open from Easter to October (see board for details).

Ickworth Church.

St. Mary - 13th century chancel of knapped flint; early 14th century nave; stuccoed west tower, and south aisle of 1833. Church silver displayed in Rotunda. (not owned by the National Trust)

Front View of Ickworth Park Hall, seat Earl of Bristol 18 Oct

THE NATIONAL TRUST

present house had been determined. In some respects the park remains more focussed on the site of the original manor house. A walk along the edge of Elizabeth Grove, a group of trees on high ground to the north of the Horringer entrance affords a number of remarkable views of the park and its buildings. Such arrangements are typical of Brown's work. Although the 'natural' appearance of the landscape today must owe much to his intervention there are many important earlier survivals. The survival of ancient pollards along the line of what must have been field boundaries, suggests that the original park at Ickworth gave way to an agricultural landscape at an early date. This field system provides a framework for the subsequent development of the landscape. The belts, planted up in the 18th century as part of the process of creating a new park, and greatly extended during the 19th century, incorporate ancient woodland (notably Lownde Wood and Dairy Wood). Interestingly the nineteenth century plantations were stocked with saplings grown on in a nursery, in contrast to the earlier forestry practice of planting seed. Ickworth is recognised as one of the most important parks in Britain for ancient specimen trees. These are chiefly old oak pollards and standards but there are also hornbeam, beech and field maple. Some of these predate the arrival of the Herveys at Ickworth.

Albana Wood.

An 18th century feature, perhaps initially laid out by 'Capability' Brown, reorganised in 1826 when the garden was established to incorporate a fine circular walk. Both wood and walk were named in honour of Elizabeth Albana Upton, the wife of the 1st Marquess. The wood, which includes both ancient and deciduous trees and a variety of evergreens planted in the nineteenth century, encompasses Round Hill, a substantial clearing which is now an enclosure for Red and Fallow deer.

Scene in Ickworth Park near Bury St Edmunds seat Earl of Bristol 18 Feb 1818

Canal.

Shortly before 1717 a canal was created on the river Linnet in an area known as Pond Close, and a walled garden and summerhouse built on the south-facing slope above it. Probably to designs by Talman, these works were presumably in anticipation of the new house intended to replace the medieval manor house.

Lakes.

A very large body of water, known as The New Canal, but in effect a reservoir, was created in the 1820s in the wide valley to the west of Albana walk. The former lake-bed is bounded to the west by Dairy Wood; the remnants of the dam can still be seen. By 1885 the lake had gone. The Fairy Lake, at the head of the Linnet seems to have been constructed at about this date.

The House.

Of the house proper only the Rotunda was nearing completion when the Earl Bishop died in Italy in 1803. The 1st Marquess constructed the curving